Macmillan McGraw-Hill

IMPACT
Mathematics

GRADE
3

Mc Graw Hill **Macmillan/McGraw-Hill**

What is IMPACT Mathematics?

Student Edition

Investigative Instruction
Hands-On Exploration with
Manipulatives and Tools

Horizontally
Aligned

Companion to Student Edition
Common Planning, Common Authors,
Common Vocabulary

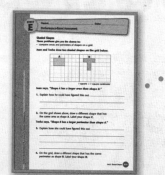

Performance-Based Assessment
See What Students Know,
Understand, and Can Do

Communication
Reasoning, Explaining,
Reflecting and Communicating

These materials include work supported in part by the National Science Foundation under Grant No. ESI-9726403 to MARS (Mathematics Assessment Resource Service). Any opinions, findings, and conclusions or recommendations expressed in this material are those of the authors and do not necessarily reflect the views of the funding agencies. For more information on MARS, visit http://www.nottingham.ac.uk/education/MARS

The **McGraw·Hill** *Companies*

Macmillan/McGraw-Hill
Glencoe

Send all inquiries to:
Macmillan/McGraw-Hill
8787 Orion Place
Columbus, OH 43240-4027

ISBN: 978-0-02-107025-1
MHID: 0-02-107025-3

Printed in the United States of America.

6 7 8 9 10   006   16 15 14 13 12 11 10 09

Contents in Brief

IMPACT Mathematics, Grade 3

Authors, Consultants, and Reviewers

About the Authors

MARS
(Mathematics Assessment Resource Services)

MARS is a U.S.-based international team of people with diverse, research-based experience in mathematics education and its performance assessment. MARS is led by its Directorate: Sandra Wilcox (Michigan State U), Hugh Burkhardt (Shell Center, Nottingham U, UK), Alan Schoenfeld and Phil Daro (UC Berkeley).

Through an NSF grant, years of development, evaluation, and research have gone into developing the high-quality, performance-based assessments at the core of **IMPACT Mathematics**.

MARS lead designer for **IMPACT Mathematics** is **Rita Crust.**

Frances Basich Whitney
Project Director, Mathematics K–12
Santa Cruz County Office of Education
Santa Cruz, California

Frances received her B.A. and M.A. from Santa Clara University. She taught mathematics for 14 years at the high school and middle school levels. In her current position, Ms. Basich Whitney provides professional development primarily for K–8 teachers and curricular support to districts throughout California.

Frances is a member of the National Council of Teachers of Mathematics and the Association for Supervision and Curriculum Development, and she is very active as a speaker and workshop leader at professional development conferences.

Robyn Silbey
Mathematics Content Coach
Montgomery County Public Schools
Gaithersburg, Maryland

Robyn has been teaching in Montgomery County, Maryland, since 1974. She is currently working as a mathematics content coach. She has authored textbooks, software, supplemental materials, and magazine and journal articles on mathematics processes and topics from Kindergarten through Algebra I.

Robyn is a national consultant and presents workshops at national and international conferences. She serves in the Teaching Training Corps for the United States Department of Education and on the editorial panel of Teaching Children Mathematics, an NCTM periodical.

About the Consultants

Macmillan/McGraw-Hill wishes to thank the following professionals for their feedback. They were instrumental in providing valuable input toward the development of this program.

Jane D. Gawronski
Director of Assessment
and Outreach
San Diego State University
San Diego, California

Viken Hovsepian
Professor of Mathematics
Rio Hondo College
Whittier, California

About the Reviewers

Each of the educators reviewed five or more units of *IMPACT Mathematics*, giving feedback and suggestions for improving the effectiveness of the mathematics instruction.

Karen H. Dillon
Mathematics Coach
Erie 1 Boces
West Seneca, New York

Sarah J. Long
Assistant Superintendent,
Curriculum/Instruction
Poplar Bluff R-I
Poplar Bluff, Missouri

LaVerne Dixon
Mathematics Coordinator
Riverview Gardens School District
St. Louis, Missouri

Karen Murray
Grade 5 Teacher
Lorraine Elementary PS #72
Buffalo, New York

Ginna Gallivan
Mentor
South Buffalo Charter School
Buffalo, New York

Deborah Schluben
Mathematics Resource Specialist
Shawnee Mission School District
Shawnee Mission, Kansas

Table of Contents

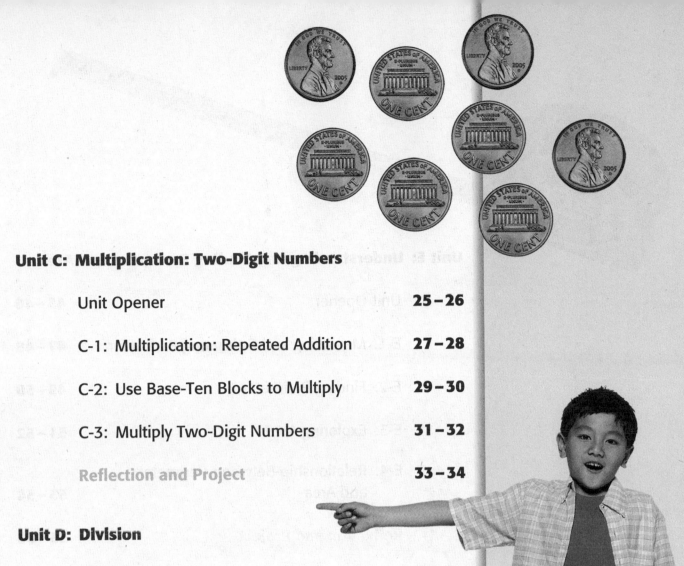

UNIT A

Multiplication— One-Digit Numbers

In this unit, I will:

- Use models or pictures to describe things that come in equal groups
- Find patterns and multiples on a hundred chart
- Explore factors for different numbers by building rectangles

Review Concepts
- multiplication, repeated addition, rectangles

Projects
- Lots of Dots Book
- Make Friendship Bracelets

New Vocabulary

area   the number of square units needed to cover the inside of a region or plane figure

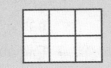

area = 6 square units

array   objects or symbols displayed in rows of the same length and columns of the same length

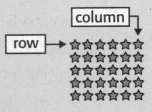

divide (division)   to separate into equal groups

equation   a sentence that contains an equals sign (=), showing that two expressions are equal

$$6 + 3 = 9$$

factor   a number that divides a whole number evenly; also a number that is multiplied by another number

$$5 \times 2 = 10$$

factors

multiple (multiples)   the *product* of that number and any whole number

multiply (multiplication)   an operation on two numbers to find their product; it can be thought of as repeated *addition*

product   the answer to a multiplication problem

one   1

Home Letter

English

During this math unit, your student will be exploring multiplication of one-digit numbers using models and drawing pictures. To help with learning, here are things to do at home.

- Look for different objects that come in equal groups (pairs of socks, wheels on a car).
- Talk about when to multiply and when to divide (finding how many pizzas to order).
- Spend time reviewing basic multiplication facts.

In class, your student will be:

- using models and pictures to solve multiplication problems;
- exploring multiples and facts on a hundred chart.

Español

Durante esta unidad de matemáticas, su estudiante va a explorar la multiplicación de números de un solo dígito por medio del uso de modelos y de hacer dibujos. Para ayudar con el aprendizaje, sugerimos estas actividades para hacer en casa:

- Busque distintos objetos que vengan en grupos iguales (pares de calcetines, las ruedas de un automóvil).
- Aclare cuándo es necesario multiplicar y cuándo es necesario dividir (para saber cuántas pizzas hay que pedir).
- Dedique tiempo a repasar las operaciones básicas de multiplicación.

En clase, su estudiante va a:

- usar modelos y dibujos para resolver problemas de multiplicación;
- explorar múltiplos y operaciones en una tabla de números hasta el cien.

Name: _____   Date: _____

Meaning of Multiplication

There are 4 people in Ray's family. Each family member wears 2 socks. He shows equal groups of 2 socks for each person in six ways:

Math Words

array

equation

multiply
(multiplication)

Array:

X X
X X
X X
X X

Repeated addition sentence: $2 + 2 + 2 + 2 = 8$
Multiplication sentence: $4 \times 2 = 8$
Word sentence: 4 groups of 2 = 8
Skip counting on a number line:

0 1 2 3 4 5 6 7 8

**Tre makes a web to show equal groups of balloons.
Complete Tre's web.**

1. 3 groups of 4 = _____
word sentence

0 1 2 3 4 5 6 7 8 9 10 11 12
number line

_____ balloons
picture

There are 3 people in my family. Each person has 4 balloons. How many balloons are there in all?

X X X X
X X X X
X X X X _____ x's
array

$3 \times 4 =$ _____
multiplication sentence

$4 + 4 + 4 =$ _____
repeated addition sentence

In Science
Did you know that insects have 6 legs? How many legs would 3 insects have? Draw a web to show your answer.

Make a web for each story.

2. _____

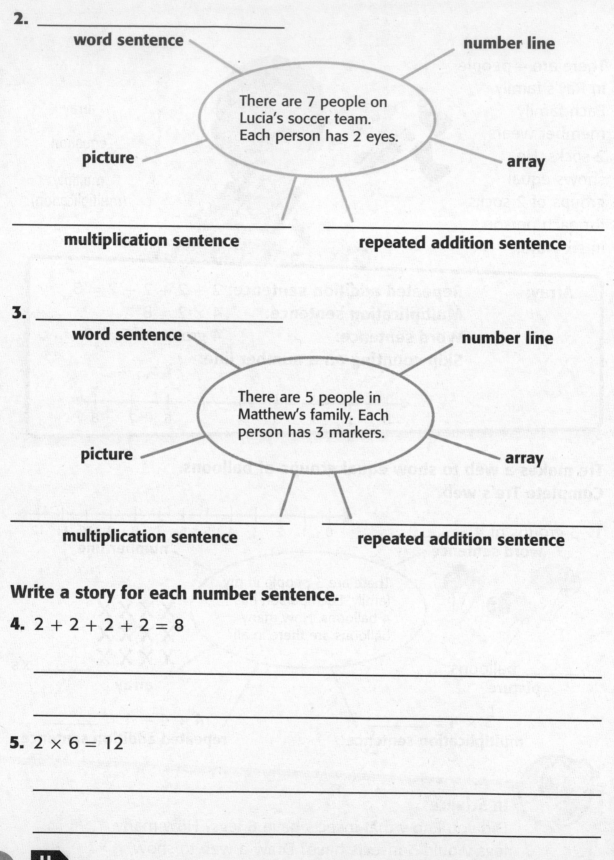

word sentence

number line

There are 7 people on Lucia's soccer team. Each person has 2 eyes.

picture

array

multiplication sentence

repeated addition sentence

3. _____

word sentence

number line

There are 5 people in Matthew's family. Each person has 3 markers.

picture

array

multiplication sentence

repeated addition sentence

Write a story for each number sentence.

4. $2 + 2 + 2 + 2 = 8$

_____

_____

5. $2 \times 6 = 12$

_____

_____

Name: _____   Date: _____

Skip Counting, Multiples, and Facts

You created a "Lots of Dots" hundred chart. Let's use the chart to explore patterns and rules for multiplication.

1	2	3	4	5	6	7	8	9	10
11	12	13	14	15	16	17	18	19	20
21	22	23	24	25	26	27	28	29	30
31	32	33	34	35	36	37	38	39	40
41	42	43	44	45	46	47	48	49	50
51	52	53	54	55	56	57	58	59	60
61	62	63	64	65	66	67	68	69	70
71	72	73	74	75	76	77	78	79	80
81	82	83	84	85	86	87	88	89	90
91	92	93	94	95	96	97	98	99	100

1. List the first 10 multiples of 5.

_____

_____

What patterns do you notice?

_____

_____

_____

2. List the 10 multiples of 10.

_____

How are the multiples of 5 and 10 related?

_____

_____

Math Words

factor

multiple

product

At Home

Which objects in your house come in groups? Are there groups of juice boxes, towels, or keys? Find at least five things that come in groups. Draw pictures of each. Use skip counting and multiples to write and solve a multiplication equation for each one.

The first multiple of 3 is where the first green dot appears on the hundred chart. Since the first multiple of 3 is 3, $1 \times 3 = 3$. Find other multiples of 3. Write the product.

3. the second multiple of 3 is _____, so $2 \times 3 =$ _____.

4. the seventh multiple of 3 is _____, so $7 \times 3 =$ _____.

5. the fourth multiple of 3 is _____, so $4 \times 3 =$ _____.

6. the ninth multiple of 3 is _____, so $9 \times 3 =$ _____.

Write a multiplication sentence for each phrase.

7. the tenth multiple of 4

_____

8. the sixth multiple of 10

_____

9. the eighth multiple of 2

_____

10. the eighth multiple of 3

_____

11. the seventh multiple of 5

_____

12. the fourth multiple of 5

_____

13. Write a story for Exercise 9.

_____

_____

Lots of Dots

Some numbers on the hundred chart, such as 20, 24, and 30, have two or more dots. What multiplication equations and pictures show what the dots mean? Create a "Lots of Dots" book showing the multiplication sentences for at least five numbers with "lots of dots." Include pictures to represent each multiplication sentence.

PROJECT

You built rectangles to show different ways to make equal groups. Let's explore more ways to use rectangles.

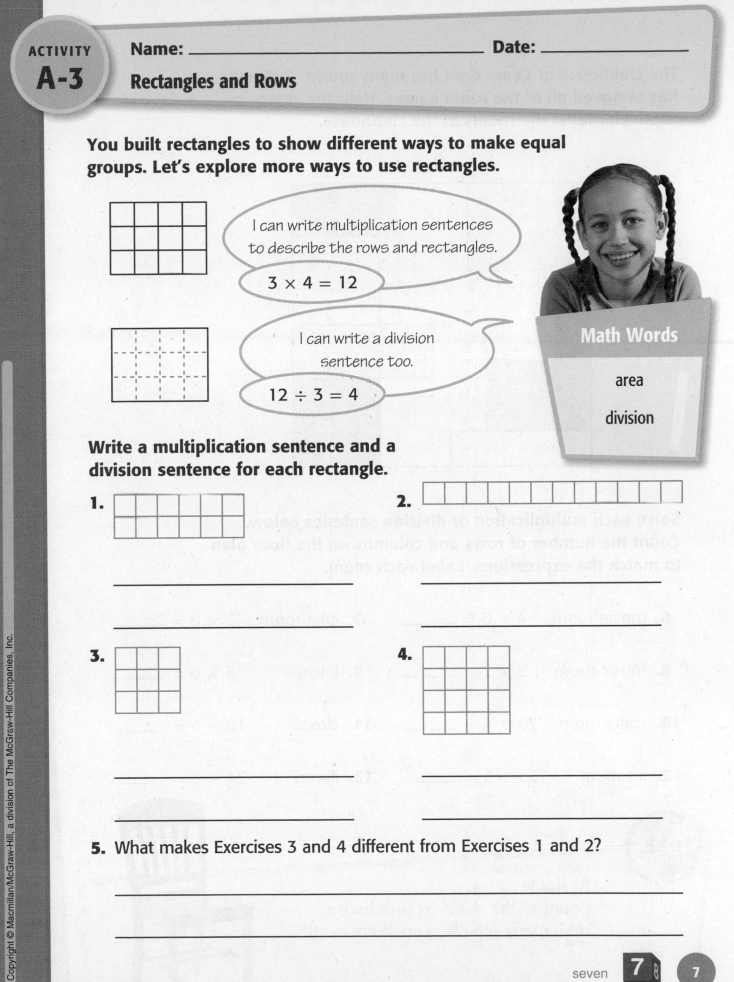

I can write multiplication sentences to describe the rows and rectangles.

$3 \times 4 = 12$

I can write a division sentence too.

$12 \div 3 = 4$

Math Words

area

division

Write a multiplication sentence and a division sentence for each rectangle.

1. _____

2. _____

3. _____

4. _____

5. What makes Exercises 3 and 4 different from Exercises 1 and 2?

_____

_____

The clubhouse at Camp Cool has many rooms. Someone has removed all of the room names. Help the camp counselor label the rooms in the clubhouse.

Club House

Solve each multiplication or division sentence below. Count the number of rows and columns on the floor plan to match the expressions. Label each room.

6. movie room $\quad 4 \times 6 =$ _____

7. coat room $\quad 2 \times 8 =$ _____

8. music room $\quad 5 \times 7 =$ _____

9. kitchen $\quad 3 \times 6 =$ _____

10. crafts room $\quad 20 \div 4 =$ _____

11. closet $\quad 10 \div 5 =$ _____

12. art room $\quad 25 \div 5 =$ _____

13. library $\quad 24 \div 3 =$ _____

At Home
Count all the chairs in your house.
How many chair legs are there in all?

Name: _____ **Date:** _____

Relating Division to Multiplication

Math Words

array

divide (division)

factor

multiply
(multiplication)

product

Juan makes model motorcycles, airplanes, and cars.
He buys a box of 24 wheels.

1. How many motorcycles can Juan build? _____

2. How many cars can Juan build? _____

3. How many airplanes can Juan build? _____

4. Put Exercises 1–3 in order from greatest to least.
Circle the items of which Juan makes the fewest.

_____ _____ _____

5. Suppose Juan wants to make a mix of motorcycles, airplanes,
and cars with the 24 wheels. What is one way he can do that?
Show your work.

_____

_____

_____

Mr. Sanchez wants to sell cold bottled water. He will need to buy a cooler to keep the water cold. There are four sizes of coolers. Each cooler can hold a different number of water bottles.

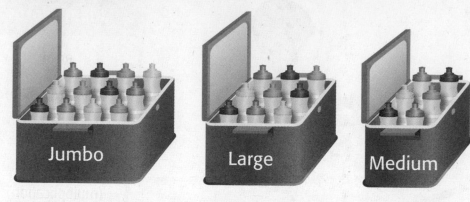

Jumbo: 12 bottles   Large: 9 bottles   Medium: 6 bottles   Small: 4 bottles

Mr. Sanchez buys 36 bottles of water. How many times will Mr. Sanchez need to fill and empty each cooler to use all 36 bottles? Show your work.

6. Jumbo _____

7. Large _____

8. Medium _____

9. Small _____

10. Explain how you figured out how many times Mr. Sanchez needed to fill and empty the small cooler.

_____

_____

11. Which cooler do you think Mr. Sanchez should buy? Explain your thinking.

_____

_____

_____

Reflecting on What I Learned

New *Vocabulary* I learned:

1. _____

2. _____

3. _____

Explain the relationship between the webs (A-1) and rectangles (A-3) you created.

_____

_____

_____

How are multiplication and division related?

_____

_____

Outside Your Classroom

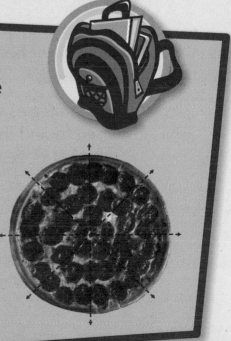

Use your multiplication and division knowledge outside the classroom.

- How many games of 4-square can be played if all of the students in your class want to play?

- How many slices of pizza are needed for your family, if each member eats 2 slices of pizza?

- How do your parents use multiplication or division at the grocery store?

Make Friendship Bracelets

In this unit, you used cubes, number lines, arrays, hundred charts, and pictures to show multiplication and division.

Use this new knowledge to create friendship bracelets for you and your friends.

1. You will use red, green, blue, and yellow beads to create a bracelet for yourself.

   ■ How many of each color bead will you use?

   ■ How many beads will you use in all?

2. Make your bracelet. Draw a picture showing what you did.

3. Look at how many beads of each color you used. Tell how many beads of each color you will need to make bracelets for 2, 3, 4, or 5 friends.

4. Write a report on your project. Include some of the following:

   ■ an explanation of the amount of beads that you used;

   ■ the strategies you used to find the number of beads needed for 2, 3, 4, and 5 friends;

   ■ how you might find out the total number of beads you need in all.

UNIT B
Patterns in Multiplication

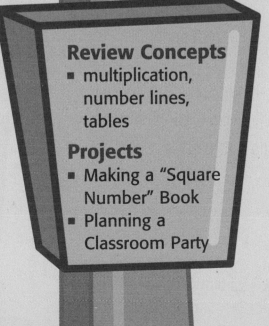

In this unit, I will:

- Use properties to multiply by 0 and 1
- Find patterns in number lines and multiplication tables
- Make function tables and use them to find patterns
- Use mental math to multiply 2-digit numbers by 1-digit numbers

Review Concepts
- multiplication, number lines, tables

Projects
- Making a "Square Number" Book
- Planning a Classroom Party

Copyright © Macmillan/McGraw-Hill, a division of The McGraw-Hill Companies, Inc.

New Vocabulary

Commutative Property of Multiplication the property that states that the order in which two numbers are multiplied does not change the product

$$7 \times 2 = 2 \times 7$$

function a relationship in which one quantity depends upon another quantity

function table a table of ordered pairs that is based on a rule

Identity Property of Multiplication if you multiply a number by 1, the product is the same as the given number

$$8 \times 1 = 8 = 1 \times 8$$

mental math adding, subtracting, multiplying, and dividing in your head

square number the product of a number multiplied by itself

Example: $5^2 = 5 \times 5 = 25$
25 is a square number

Zero Property of Multiplication the property that states any number multiplied by zero is zero

$$0 \times 5 = 0 \qquad 5 \times 0 = 0$$

thirteen XXXXXXXXXX XXX 13

Home Letter

English

During this math unit, your student will be exploring properties of multiplication, patterns, and function tables and using mental math to multiply.

To help with learning, here are things to do at home.

- Look for situations in everyday life where one amount is dependent upon another (for example, bicycle wheels and number of bicycles).
- Find examples of real-life situations in which you would need to multiply by 0 and 1, for example, 3 egg cartons each with 0 eggs $(3 \times 0 = 0)$ and eating 1 apple every day for a week $(7 \times 1 = 7)$.

In class, your student will be:

- learning to multiply with 1 and 0;
- creating function tables and looking for patterns;
- mentally multiplying 2-digit numbers by 1-digit numbers.

Español

Durante esta unidad de matemáticas, su estudiante va a explorar las propiedades de multiplicación, patrones, y tablas de función y a usar cálculo mental para multiplicar. Para ayudar con el aprendizaje, sugerimos estas actividades para hacer en casa:

- Busque situaciones de la vida diaria en que una cantidad dependa de otra (por ejemplo: ruedas de bicicleta y número de bicicletas).
- Encuentre ejemplos de situaciones de la vida diaria en que se necesitaría multiplicar por 0 y 1, por ejemplo: 3 cartones de huevos, cada uno con 0 huevos $(3 \times 0 = 0)$ y comer una manzana al día durante una semana $(7 \times 1 = 7)$.

En clase, su estudiante va a:

- aprender a multiplicar con 1 y 0;
- crear tablas de función y buscar patrones;
- multiplicar mentalmente números de dos dígitos por números de 1 dígito.

Name: _____ Date: _____

Multiply by 1 and 0

Let's explore more about multiplication facts with 0 and 1.

There are 5 boxes of crayons. Each box has 1 crayon in it. There are 4 boxes of markers. Each box has 0 markers. The special properties below can help to find the total number of crayons and the total number of markers.

Math Words

Identity Property of Multiplication

Zero Property of Multiplication

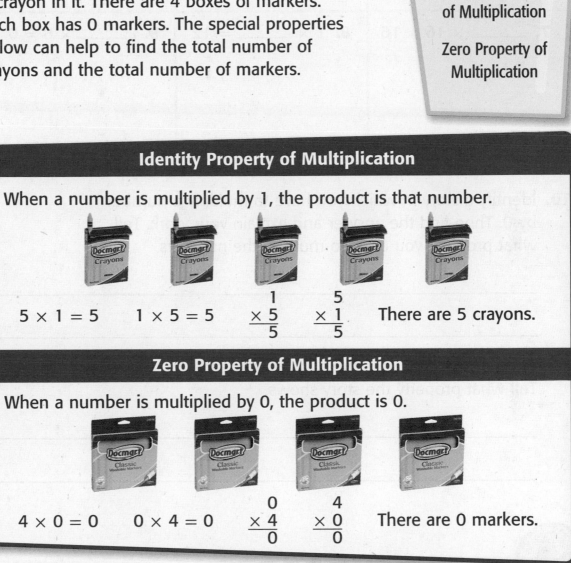

Identity Property of Multiplication

When a number is multiplied by 1, the product is that number.

$5 \times 1 = 5$ $1 \times 5 = 5$ $\begin{array}{r} 1 \\ \times 5 \\ \hline 5 \end{array}$ $\begin{array}{r} 5 \\ \times 1 \\ \hline 5 \end{array}$ There are 5 crayons.

Zero Property of Multiplication

When a number is multiplied by 0, the product is 0.

$4 \times 0 = 0$ $0 \times 4 = 0$ $\begin{array}{r} 0 \\ \times 4 \\ \hline 0 \end{array}$ $\begin{array}{r} 4 \\ \times 0 \\ \hline 0 \end{array}$ There are 0 markers.

Write the property that each number sentence shows.

1. $1 \times 7 = 7$ **2.** $0 \times 2 = 2$ **3.** $9 \times 1 = 9$

_____   _____   _____

_____   _____   _____

Use properties to find the missing number. Identify the property.

4. $10 \times \underline{\hspace{1cm}} = 0$	**5.** $5 \times 0 = \underline{\hspace{1cm}}$	**6.** $\underline{\hspace{1cm}} \times 1 = 4$
7. $\underline{\hspace{1cm}} \times 16 = 16$	**8.** $1 \times \underline{\hspace{1cm}} = 12$	**9.** $\underline{\hspace{1cm}} \times 8 = 0$

10. Identify a story in which you have to multiply a number by 0. Then find the answer and explain your work. Tell what property you used to multiply the numbers.

_____

_____

11. Write a story that uses the number sentence $25 \times 1 = 25$. Tell what property the story shows.

_____

_____

In Social Studies

Did you know that someone who collects coins is called a numismatist? You can be a numismatist, too! Look around your house for different coins. Make a sketch of the coins. Then design a coin book. Tell how many pages you would need to display your coins if you put 1 coin on each page.

Name: _____ Date: _____

Multiplication Tables

Use a multiplication table to find patterns.

1. Make a multiplication table through 10 × 10. Use it to find the multiples of 4 and 10.

_____

_____

_____

2. How is using a multiplication table to find multiples different than using a number line? _____

_____

_____

3. Find 3 × 6 and 6 × 3 on the multiplication table. What do you notice about the products? What property does this show?

_____

_____

4. Circle all of the 8s on the multiplication table. How many are there? Why is this so?

_____

_____

_____

_____

×	0	1	2	3	4	5	6	7	8	9	10
0	0	0	0	0	0	0	0	0	0	0	0
1	0	1	2	3	4	5	6	7	8	9	10
2	0	2	4	6	8	10	12	14	16	18	20
3	0	3	6	9	12	15	18	21	24	27	30
4	0	4	8	12	16	20	24	28	32	36	40
5	0	5	10	15	20	25	30	35	40	45	50
6	0	6	12	18	24	30	36	42	48	54	60
7	0	7	14	21	28	35	42	49	56	63	70
8	0	8	16	24	32	40	48	56	64	72	80
9	0	9	18	27	36	45	54	63	72	81	90
10	0	10	20	30	40	50	60	70	80	90	100

If you multiply a factor by itself, the product is called a *square number*. In your multiplication table, shade the boxes for 1, 4, 9, and 16. These numbers are square numbers.

5. What number sentences show that these numbers are square numbers?

_____

6. What other square numbers are on the multiplication table? How can you find them? _____

_____

_____

7. What pattern do the square numbers make on the multiplication table?

_____

_____

Describe any patterns you find in the multiples of the numbers below.

8. 0 _____   **9.** 5 _____

_____   _____

"Square Number" Book

Use grid paper to show a 2 × 2 grid. Count the grid squares. There are 4 grid squares, so this grid represents the square number 4. Cut out the grid and tape it to the first page of your book. Write *Square Number: 4; Number Sentence: 2 × 2 = 4*. Make a page for as many square numbers as you can. Include the grid paper model, the square number, and the corresponding number sentence.

In the investigation, you found patterns by modeling pyramid towers.

Now you will use function tables to find patterns.

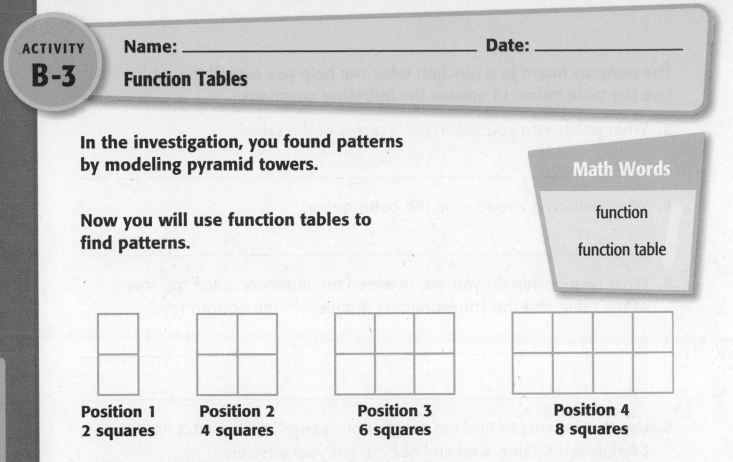

Position 1
2 squares

Position 2
4 squares

Position 3
6 squares

Position 4
8 squares

Look at the pattern of squares above. Draw the next 2 figures in the pattern. Then complete the function table.

1.

Position 5

2.

Position 6

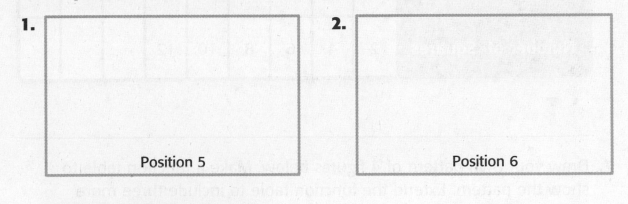

Position of Figure	1	2	3	4	5	6
Number of Squares	2	4	6	8		

The patterns found in a function table can help you extend the table. Use the table below to answer the following questions.

3. What pattern do you see in the top row of the table?

_____

4. What pattern do you see in the bottom row?

_____

5. What relationship do you see between the numbers in the top row of the table and the corresponding numbers in the bottom row?

_____

_____

6. Use the patterns to find the number of squares in the next 3 figures. Complete the table. Explain how you got your answers.

Position of Figure	1	2	3	4	5	6			
Number of Squares	2	4	6	8	10	12			

_____

7. Draw your own pattern of 4 figures below. Make a function table to show the pattern. Extend the function table to include three more figures in the pattern. Sketch the figures below.

OOOOOOOOOO twenty
OOOOOOOOOO

In the investigation, you used grids to find different ways to multiply 4 × 8. Now you will use grids and mental math to multiply 2-digit numbers by 1-digit numbers.

Use mental math to multiply 4 × 13.

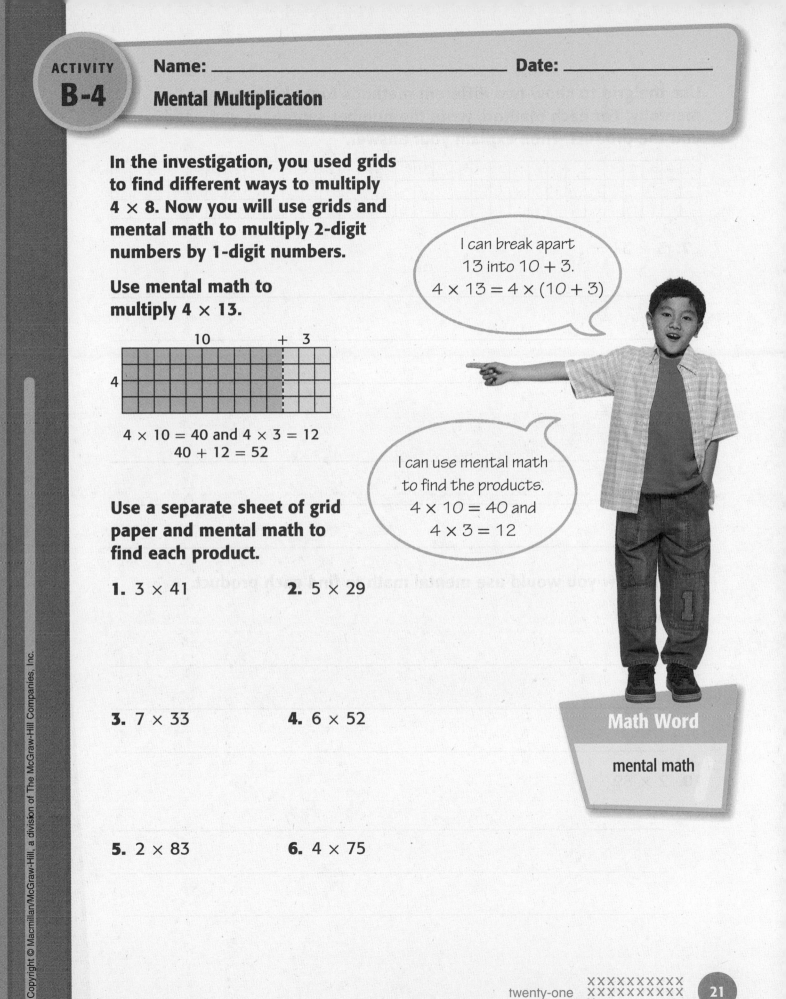

10   + 3

4

$4 \times 10 = 40$ and $4 \times 3 = 12$
$40 + 12 = 52$

I can break apart 13 into 10 + 3.
$4 \times 13 = 4 \times (10 + 3)$

I can use mental math to find the products.
$4 \times 10 = 40$ and $4 \times 3 = 12$

Use a separate sheet of grid paper and mental math to find each product.

1. 3 × 41

2. 5 × 29

3. 7 × 33

4. 6 × 52

5. 2 × 83

6. 4 × 75

Math Word

mental math

Use the grid to show two different methods to multiply 3 × 31 mentally. For each method, write the number sentences you used and the product. Then explain your answer.

7. 3 × 31 =

_____

_____

_____

8. 3 × 31 =

_____

_____

_____

Explain how you would use mental math to find each product.

9. 6 × 47

_____

_____

_____

10. 2 × 89

_____

_____

_____

Reflecting on What I Learned

New *Vocabulary* I learned:

1. _____

_____

2. _____

_____

3. _____

_____

How can you use mental math to multiply?

_____

_____

What is significant about multiplying by 1? By 0? _____

_____

_____

Outside Your Classroom

What examples of functions do you see around you?

- Find a pattern in your home (number of books on shelves). Describe and sketch the pattern. If possible, extend the pattern.

- Describe one situation when you might need to multiply a two-digit by one-digit number. Explain how you could use addends and mental math to solve.

Planning a Classroom Party

PROJECT

Use your knowledge of patterns and function tables to plan a classroom party. Your plan should include food, games, and party gifts.

1. Decide what food you will need for the party.

- Make a list of the food items you will need.

- Include the correct number of each item for the number of students in your class. (Don't forget your teacher!)

- Use function tables to help you plan. For example, if you want everyone to have 2 snacks and there are 12 people in the class, the function table might look like this.

People	1	2	3	4	5	6	7	8	9	10	11	12
Snacks	2	4	6	8	10	12	14	16	18	20	22	24

2. Decide what games you will play.

- Consider how much time you have and how long each game takes.

- Describe how you can use a function table like the one below to help you plan the games.

Game	1			
Time	15	30	45	60

3. Decide what other supplies you might need, such as prizes and decorations. How can you break apart the number of students to use mental multiplication?

4. Write a report that summarizes your plan. Include the following:

- how you used the math from this unit to plan the party;
- the food, games, and prizes that you intend to include.

UNIT C

Multiplication— Two-Digit Numbers

In this unit, I will:

- Relate multiplication to repeated addition
- Use base-ten blocks to multiply two-digit numbers by one-digit numbers
- Use paper and pencil to record multiplication problems

Review Concepts
- basic multiplication facts, place value

Projects
- Make an "I Know How to Multiply" Poster
- Make an *Animal Facts* Book

Review Vocabulary

factor   a number that is multiplied by another number

multiplication   an operation on two numbers to find their product; it can be thought of as *repeated addition*

product   the answer to a multiplication problem

Home Letter

English

During this math unit, your student will explore ways to multiply two-digit numbers by one-digit numbers. To help with learning, here are things to do at home.

- Point out different numbers found in the newspaper or on TV. Ask students to identify the number of digits in the number.
- Review basic multiplication facts.
- Discuss when you would need to multiply two-digit by one-digit numbers (buying 12 pencils for 5¢ each).

In class, your student will be:

- modeling multiplication using base-ten blocks;
- using paper and pencil to find the product of multiplication problems involving greater two-digit numbers.

Español

Durante esta unidad de matemáticas, su estudiante va a explorar las maneras de multiplicar números de dos dígitos por números de un solo dígito. Para ayudar con el aprendizaje, sugerimos estas actividades para hacer en casa.

- Señale los distintos números que se encuentran en el periódico o en la TV. Pídale a su estudiante que identifique cuántos dígitos hay en dichos números.
- Repase las operaciones de multiplicación básicas.
- Comente cuándo necesitaría multiplicar números de dos dígitos por números de un solo dígito (al comprar 12 lápices a 5 ¢ cada uno).

En clase, su estudiante va a:

- dar ejemplos de multiplicación con bloques de base diez;
- usar papel y lápiz para hallar el producto de problemas de multiplicación que involucran números mayores de dos dígitos.

Name: _____ **Date:** _____

Multiplication: Repeated Addition

In the investigation, you used base-ten blocks to show the relationship between repeated addition and multiplication. Now you can multiply two-digit numbers.

Math Words

factor

multiplication

product

$3 \times 24 = ?$

$24 + 24 + 24 = ?$

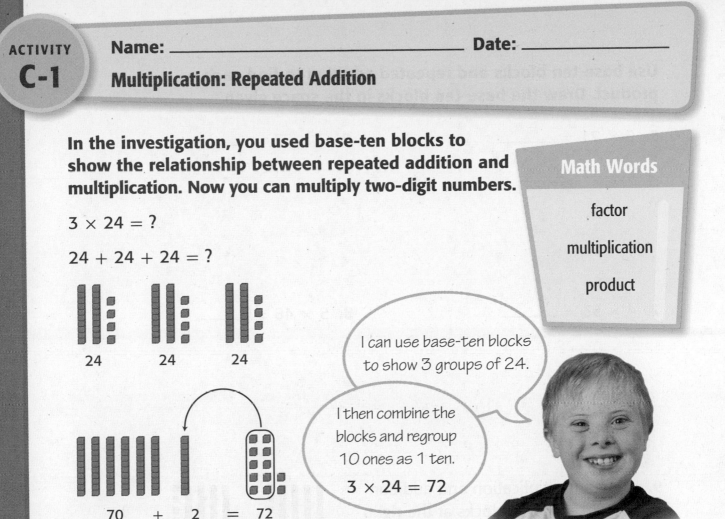

24   24   24

70   +   2   =   72

I can use base-ten blocks to show 3 groups of 24.

I then combine the blocks and regroup 10 ones as 1 ten.

$3 \times 24 = 72$

Write an addition expression and a multiplication expression for each group of base-ten blocks.

1.

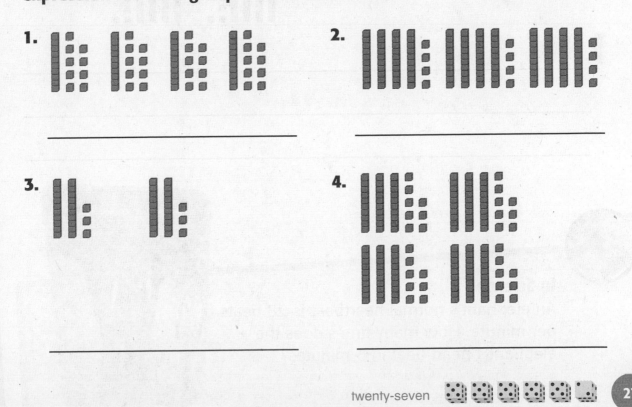

2.

_____

3.

4.

_____

Use base-ten blocks and repeated addition to find each product. Draw the base-ten blocks in the space given.

5. $6 \times 21 =$ _____

6. $2 \times 83 =$ _____

7. $4 \times 53 =$ _____

8. $5 \times 48 =$ _____

9. Write a multiplication and addition sentence for the blocks at the right. Then write a story that uses the number sentence.

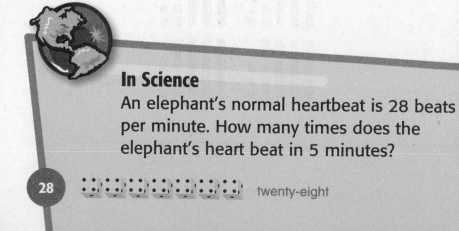

_____

_____

_____

In Science
An elephant's normal heartbeat is 28 beats per minute. How many times does the elephant's heart beat in 5 minutes?

In the investigation, you used base-ten blocks to multiply.
Now use paper and pencil to record the multiplication steps.

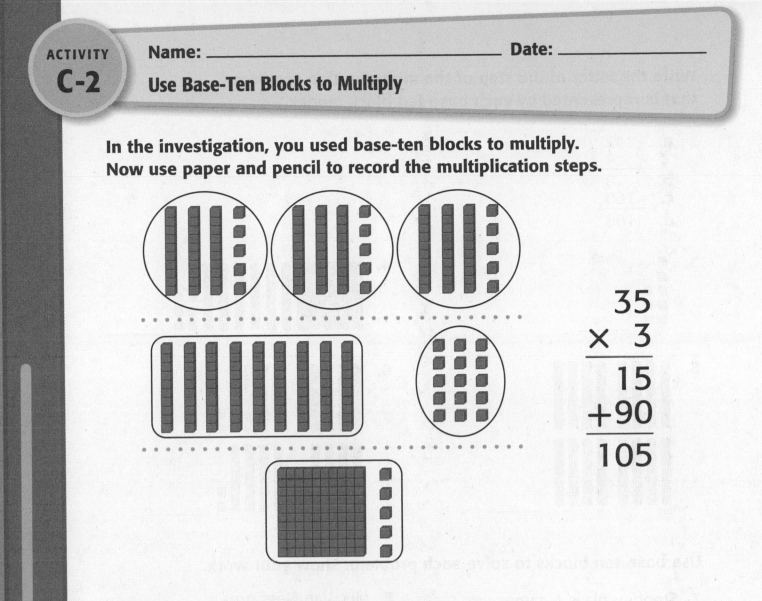

$$
\begin{array}{r}
35 \\
\times\ 3 \\
\hline
15 \\
+90 \\
\hline
105
\end{array}
$$

Use base-ten blocks to model each product.
Explain how the blocks show the multiplication steps.

1.
$$
\begin{array}{r}
44 \\
\times\ 5 \\
\hline
20 \\
+200 \\
\hline
220
\end{array}
$$

_____

_____

_____

2.
$$
\begin{array}{r}
23 \\
\times\ 8 \\
\hline
24 \\
+160 \\
\hline
184
\end{array}
$$

_____

_____

_____

Write the letter of the step of the multiplication problem that is represented by each base-ten block model.

a. 42
    × 4
b.   8
c. +160
d.   168

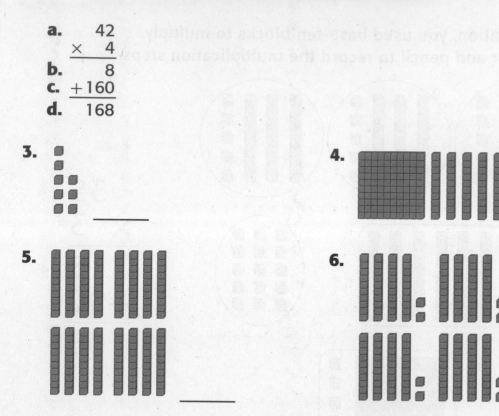

3. _____

4. _____

5. _____

6. _____

Use base-ten blocks to solve each problem. Show your work.

7. Stephen plays 4 games with his sister. Each game lasts 35 minutes. How many minutes do Stephen and his sister play games?

_____

8. Mrs. Van Ness runs 8 miles every day for 3 weeks. How many miles does she run?

_____

Name: _____ **Date:** _____

Multiply Two-Digit Numbers

Use what you know about multiplication to multiply using paper and pencil.

$$\begin{array}{r} \overset{5}{8}6 \\ \times\ 9 \\ \hline 774 \end{array}$$

I multiply the ones.
9 × 6 ones = 54 ones
I write **4** and regroup **5** tens.

Then I multiply the tens and add the regrouped tens.
9 × 8 tens = 72 tens
+ 5 tens = 77 tens

I write **77** next to the **4**.
The product is **774**.

Solve each multiplication problem represented by the base-ten blocks. Show your work.

1.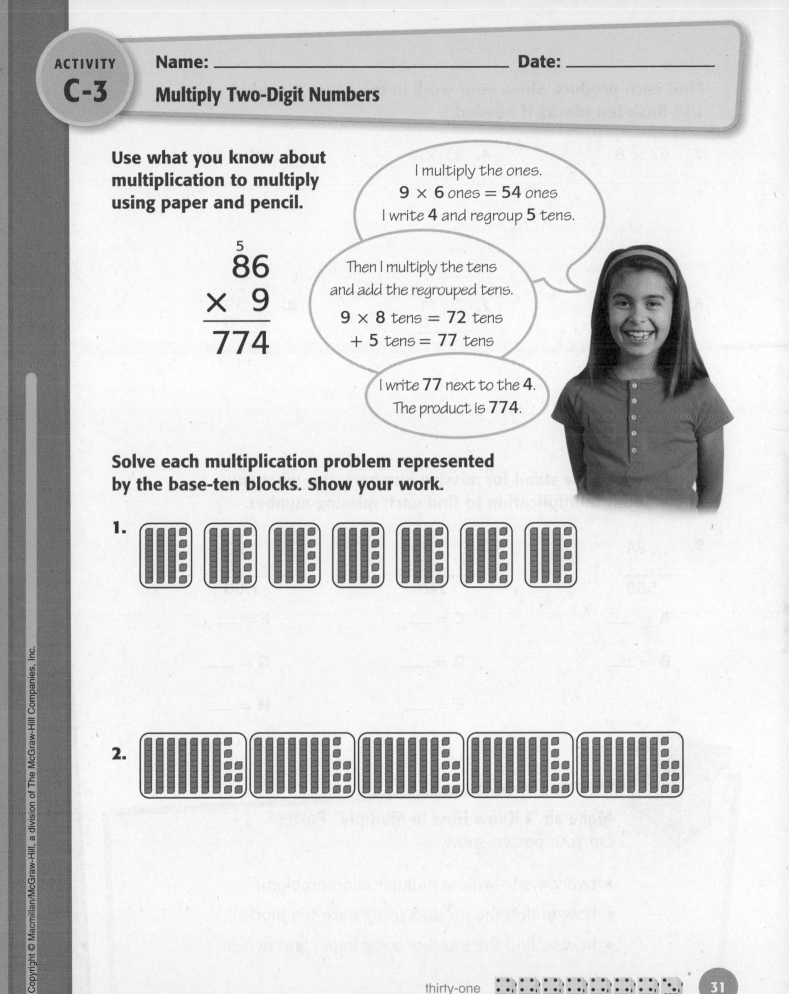

2.

**Find each product. Show your work in the space provided.
Use base-ten blocks if needed.**

3. 67 × 8

4. 93 × 7

5. 69 × 5

6.
$$\begin{array}{r} 97 \\ \times\ \ 9 \\ \hline \end{array}$$

7.
$$\begin{array}{r} 74 \\ \times\ \ 6 \\ \hline \end{array}$$

8.
$$\begin{array}{r} 39 \\ \times\ \ 8 \\ \hline \end{array}$$

**The letters below stand for missing numbers. Use what you
know about multiplication to find each missing number.**

9.
$$\begin{array}{r} \overset{2}{8}A \\ \times\ \ 7 \\ \hline 5B8 \end{array}$$

A = ___

B = ___

10.
$$\begin{array}{r} \overset{C}{D}7 \\ \times\ \ 6 \\ \hline 34E \end{array}$$

C = ___

D = ___

E = ___

11.
$$\begin{array}{r} \overset{F}{9}G \\ \times\ \ 8 \\ \hline H60 \end{array}$$

F = ___

G = ___

H = ___

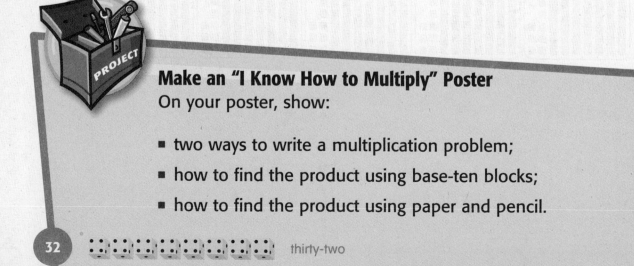

Make an "I Know How to Multiply" Poster
On your poster, show:

- two ways to write a multiplication problem;
- how to find the product using base-ten blocks;
- how to find the product using paper and pencil.

Reflecting on What I Learned

New *Vocabulary* I learned:

1. _____

2. _____

3. _____

Explain how multiplication is like repeated addition.

_____

_____

_____

Name one way to multiply a two-digit number by a one-digit number.

_____

_____

Outside Your Classroom

- How could you use repeated addition to find the total number of baseballs in a collection that is displayed in 5 cases with 32 balls in each?

- How could base-ten blocks help you multiply to find the number of cards in several decks of cards?

- How could you use pencil and paper to multiply if you wanted to buy 75¢ hotdogs for you and two friends?

Make an *Animal Facts* Book

In this unit, you multiplied two-digit by one-digit numbers. Use this new knowledge to make a book about animals.

Animal Heart Rates		Animal Speed		Animal Height	
Animal	Normal Heart Rate (beats per minute)	Animal	Maximum Speed (miles per hour)	Animal	Height
Large dog	75	Large dog	19	Large dog	28 in.
Horse	44	Horse	48	Horse	72 in.
Giraffe	67	Giraffe	30	Giraffe	16 ft
Human	62	Human	28	Human	66 in.

Make a page for each animal. Use markers or colored pencils to draw the animal, cut out pictures from magazines, or print pictures from the Internet.

1. Write statements about the animal using the facts given. Solve two-digit by one-digit multiplication problems to write the statements, for example:

   - The _____'s heart would beat _____ times in _____ minutes.

2. On the last page of your book, write comparison problems using your animal facts.

3. Write a report on your project. Include some of the following:

   - What other facts did you include and how did you gather the information?

   - What methods did you use to multiply?

UNIT D

Division

In this unit, I will:

- Relate division to repeated subtraction
- Divide with arrays using grid paper and counters
- Explore the relationship between division and fractions

Review Concepts

- multiplication
- fractions
- arrays

Projects

- Counter Arrays
- Make a Personal Scrapbook

New Vocabulary

area   the number of square units needed to cover the inside of a region or plane figure

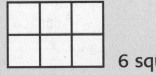

6 square units

divide (division)   to separate into equal groups

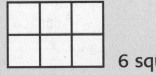

quotient   remainder

$$3\overline{)425} = 141 \text{ R2}$$

divisor ⟶ 3)425

dividend

fraction   a number that represents part of a whole or part of a set

denominator ⟶ $\dfrac{3}{4}$ ⟵ numerator

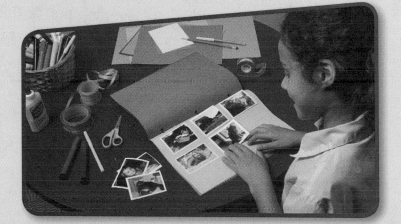

Home Letter

English

During this math unit, your student will be exploring division. To help with learning, here are things to do at home.

- Point out situations where you need to divide something into equal parts or groups.
- Look for objects around your house, in the playground, or at the store that show examples of arrays (for example, window panes or display cases). Have your student explain how the object shows multiplication and division facts.

In class, your student will be:

- relating division to repeated subtraction and equal groups;
- modeling division using arrays made with grid paper and counters;
- exploring how division and fractions are related.

Español

Durante esta unidad de matemáticas, su estudiante va a explorar la división. Para ayudar con el aprendizaje, sugerimos estas actividades para hacer en casa:

- Indique situaciones en las que necesita dividir algo en partes o grupos iguales.
- Busque objetos en su casa, en el parque de juegos o en la tienda que muestren ejemplos de arreglos, por ejemplo: cristales de ventanas o vitrinas. Pídale a su estudiante que explique de qué manera el objeto muestra las operaciones de multiplicación y división.

En clase, su estudiante va a:

- relacionar la división con la resta repetida y los grupos iguales;
- dar ejemplos de división por medio de arreglos hechos con papel cuadriculado y fichas;
- explorar de qué manera se relacionan la división y las fracciones.

Name: _____ Date: _____

Division: Repeated Subtraction

Use counters and repeated subtraction to explore division.

Jeff places 15 counters into equal groups of 5. Each time he places 5 counters, he subtracts 5 from the total number of counters.

15 counters $15 - 5 = 10$ $10 - 5 = 5$ $5 - 5 = 0$

$15 \div 5 = 3$

So, 15 counters divided into groups of 5 is 3. There are 3 groups of 5.

Draw counters and complete the number sentences to solve.

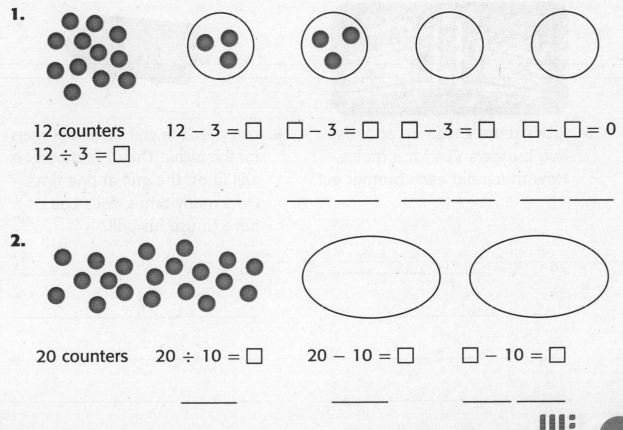

1.

12 counters $12 - 3 = \square$ $\square - 3 = \square$ $\square - 3 = \square$ $\square - \square = 0$

$12 \div 3 = \square$

_____   _____   _____   _____   _____

2.

20 counters $20 \div 10 = \square$ $20 - 10 = \square$ $\square - 10 = \square$

_____   _____   _____

Use repeated subtraction to find each quotient. Write the number sentences you used.

3. At the pool, there are 18 towels that need to be folded. There are 6 people working. How many towels does each person need to fold?

18 ÷ 6 = _____

_____

_____

4. Jamie earns $49.00 a week for mowing grass. How much is that per day?

49 ÷ 7 = _____

_____

_____

5. Rick's mom gave him and his two brothers $24 for a movie. How much did each brother get?

24 ÷ 3 = _____

_____

_____

6. Lou needs to grill 56 hamburgers for the picnic. Only 7 hamburgers will fit on the grill at one time. How many times does Lou have to use his grill?

56 ÷ 7 = _____

_____

_____

Name: _____ Date: _____

Division Using Arrays

In the investigation, you used arrays to show division. Now explore more about arrays and division.

Which number has more factors? Draw grid arrays to solve.

1. 24 or 36 _____

2. 12 or 19 _____

3. 15 or 25 _____

4. 10 or 29 _____

5. 32 or 46 _____

6. 16 or 27 _____

7. Maria says that the number 24 has more factors than 20. Is she correct? Explain your reasoning.

_____

_____

_____

Use counter arrays to find each quotient.

8. $56 \div 8$ **9.** $72 \div 9$ **10.** $16 \div 4$

_____   _____   _____

11. $49 \div 7$ **12.** $36 \div 3$ **13.** $24 \div 6$

_____   _____   _____

Write the division sentence represented by each grid array.
Then use other arrays to find all the factors of the dividend.

14.

_____

_____

15.

_____

_____

16.

_____

_____

17.

_____

_____

Counter Arrays
Choose a number greater than 50. Use counter arrays to find all the factors of your number. Sketch the arrays and explain your work using number sentences. Display your work.

Name: _____ Date: _____

Division: Preparing for Fractions

Josiah has cherry pies to share with his friends.

Use fraction circles to write each quotient as a fraction. Draw a picture to show your answer.

1. Josiah shares 1 pie with 3 other friends. What fraction of the pie does each friend get?

   $1 \div 4$ _____

2. Now Josiah shares 2 pies with his 3 friends. What fraction of the pies does each friend get?

   $2 \div 4$ _____

3. If Josiah shares 1 pie with 5 other friends, what fraction of the pie does each person get?

   $1 \div 6$ _____

4. If he shares 2 pies with his 5 friends, what fraction does each friend get?

   $2 \div 6$ _____

5. Loricia baked 3 cherry pies. She wants to share the pies equally among her 10 friends. How much pie will each friend get? Draw a picture to show your work. Write a division sentence to show the answer.

_____

6. Write a story problem that can be solved using the division expression 8 ÷ 4. Then write a story problem that can be solved using 4 ÷ 8. Solve and explain the answers to your problems. Use fraction circles to help you.

_____

_____

_____

_____

In the Kitchen

Natalie uses 3 teaspoons of food coloring to make a batch of cookies. There are 12 cookies in a batch. What division sentence shows how many teaspoons of food coloring are in each cookie? Look around your kitchen and in recipes for other things you have to divide to use. Describe some examples. Use a division sentence to represent each example.

Reflecting on What I Learned

New *Vocabulary* I learned:

1. _____

2. _____

3. _____

Explain how division is like repeated subtraction.

_____

_____

_____

_____

Outside Your Classroom

Where do you see division outside the classroom?

- How could you use repeated subtraction to show how to share peanuts equally with friends?

- Explain why this grid is not an array.

- How could you use fractions to describe how to share an item if you do not have enough for everyone?

Make a Personal Scrapbook

Use your knowledge of arrays, repeated subtraction, division, and fractions to make a scrapbook.

1. Decide how many photos or drawings you want to put in your scrapbook. Decide how many pages you will need in your scrapbook.

   ■ Are all your pictures the same size?

   ■ How many pictures will you put on a page?

2. Decide what other materials you will need to decorate your scrapbook.

   ■ Are you going to use borders?

   ■ How can you use counters or arrays to model the layout?

3. Write division sentences and fractions to show and describe your work.

   ■ How can division help you find out how many pictures you need to fit on a page, or how many pages you need?

   ■ What fraction of a page is one picture? What fraction of the scrapbook is one page? What fraction of the scrapbook is one picture?

4. Write a report about your project. Include some of the following:

   ■ What materials did you use in your scrapbook?

   ■ What division sentences helped you plan your scrapbook?

   ■ How did you use fractions to describe your scrapbook?

UNIT E

Exploring Perimeter and Area

In this unit, I will:

- Make and use my own ruler
- Find the perimeter of classroom objects using my ruler
- Record various perimeters in my "Perimeter Book"
- Find the area of classroom objects

Review Concepts

- inches, centimeters, feet, meters, ruler

Projects

- Creating a "Perimeter Book"
- Designing an "Outside Space"

New Vocabulary

area the number of square units needed to cover the inside of a plane figure

The area is 9.

base *side* of a *figure* that is used to find its height by drawing a line from the opposite angle

height distance from bottom to top

perimeter the distance around a shape or region

ruler a measuring tool used to find the length of an object

Home Letter

English

During this math unit, your student will be exploring perimeter and area with standard and nonstandard measuring tools. To help with learning, here are things to do at home.

- Look at measuring devices around the house (measuring tape, ruler, and so on). Use a combination of feet/inches and meters/centimeters.
- Talk about when you have measured objects and the reason you measured.
- Spend time estimating the length of objects. Measure to see how accurate you are.

In class, your student will be:

- creating their own ruler (to understand units of measure);
- using color tiles to explore area.

Español

Durante esta unidad de matemáticas, su estudiante va a explorar el perímetro y el área con herramientas de medición estándar y no estándar. Para ayudar con el aprendizaje, sugerimos estas actividades para hacer en casa:

- Examine instrumentos de medición alrededor de su casa (cinta métrica, regla y demás). Utilice una combinación de pies/pulgadas y metros/centímetros.
- Hable acerca de cuándo usted ha medido objetos y del motivo para medirlos.
- Dedique tiempo a estimar la longitud de varios objetos. Luego, mídalos para saber cuán precisa fue su estimación.

En clases su estudiante va a:

- crear su propia regla (para entender las unidades de medición);
- usar fichas de colores para explorar el área.

Name: _____ Date: _____

Measuring and Estimating Perimeter

Use your measuring tools and estimation skills for the following.

1. List four objects that are about 12 inches long.

_____   _____

_____   _____

2. List two objects that are about 6 inches long.

_____

_____

Order from greatest to least perimeter.

3.

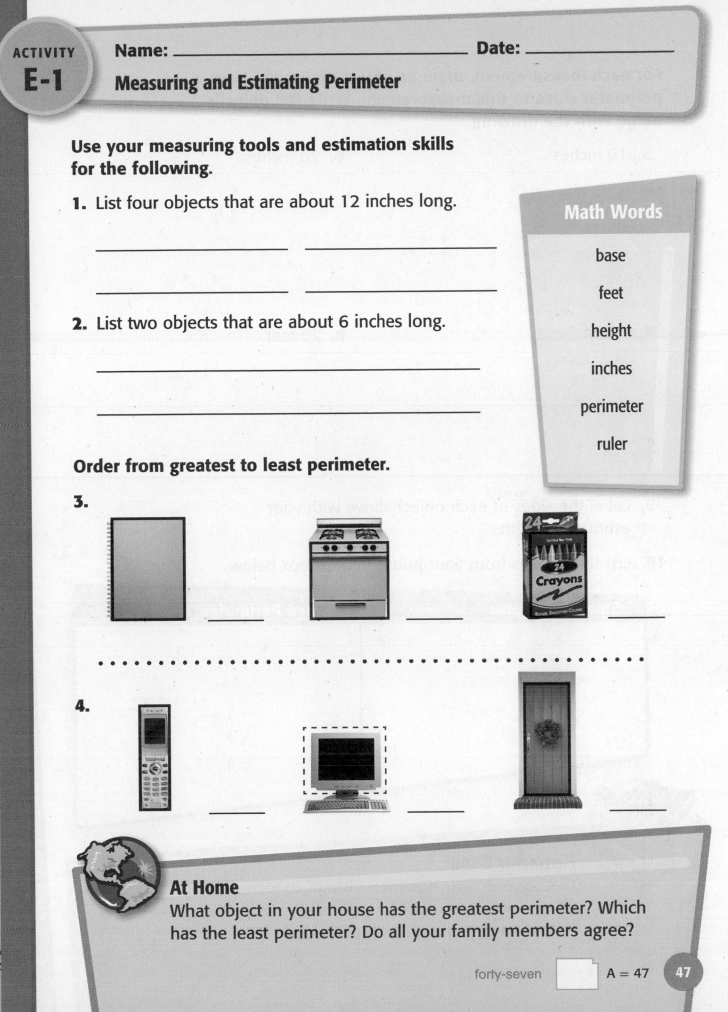

· ·

4.

Math Words

base

feet

height

inches

perimeter

ruler

At Home
What object in your house has the greatest perimeter? Which has the least perimeter? Do all your family members agree?

For each measurement, draw an object that might have a perimeter close to this measurement. Write the object's name with the drawing.

5. 10 inches

6. 20 inches

7. 1 foot

8. 20 feet

9. Label the sides of each object above with your estimated lengths.

10. List three items from your house in each box below.

Small Perimeter	Large Perimeter

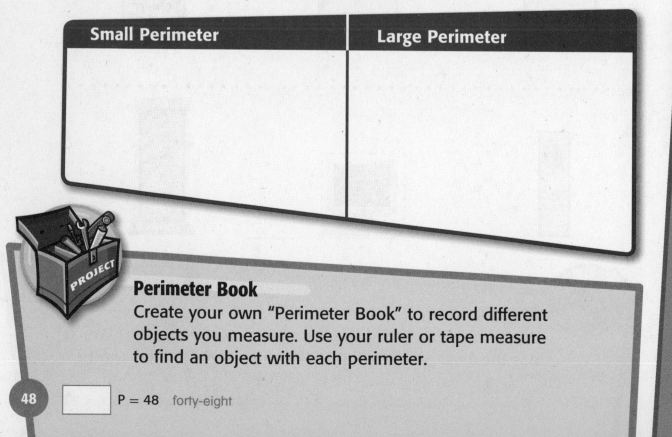

Perimeter Book
Create your own "Perimeter Book" to record different objects you measure. Use your ruler or tape measure to find an object with each perimeter.

Name: _____ Date: _____

Finding Perimeter

You have measured many objects and recorded them in your Perimeter Book. Let's explore calculating perimeter.

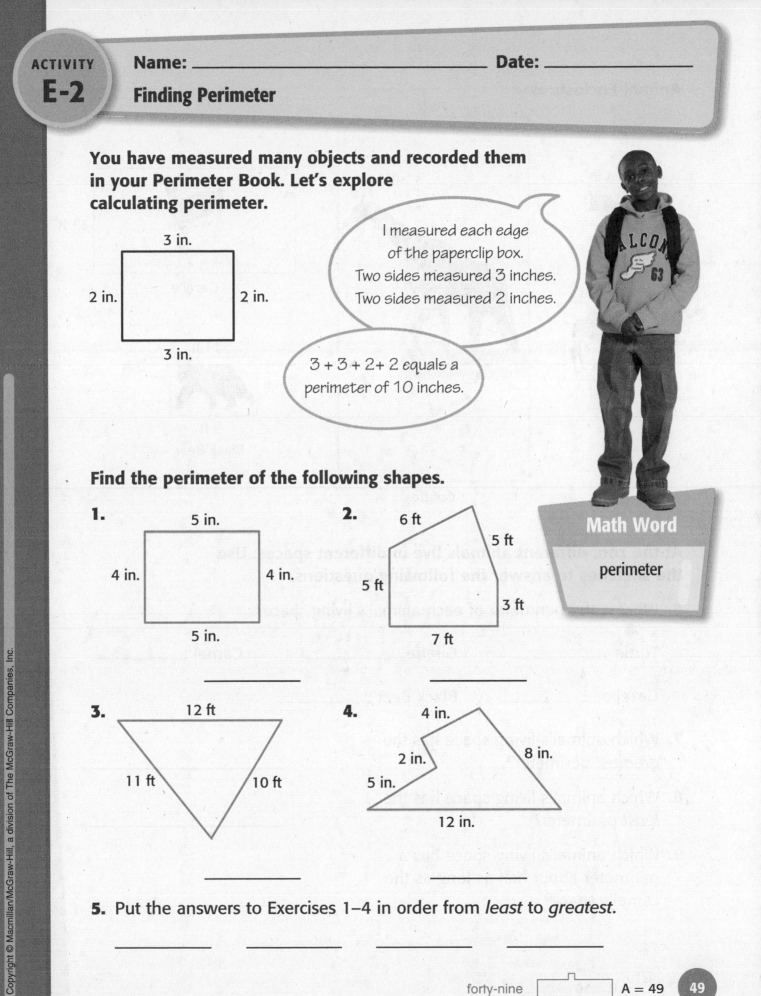

3 in.

2 in.   2 in.

3 in.

I measured each edge of the paperclip box. Two sides measured 3 inches. Two sides measured 2 inches.

3 + 3 + 2 + 2 equals a perimeter of 10 inches.

Math Word

perimeter

Find the perimeter of the following shapes.

1.
5 in.

4 in.   4 in.

5 in.

_____

2.
6 ft

5 ft

5 ft

3 ft

7 ft

_____

3.
12 ft

11 ft   10 ft

_____

4.
4 in.

2 in.   8 in.

5 in.

12 in.

_____

5. Put the answers to Exercises 1–4 in order from *least* to *greatest*.

_____ _____ _____ _____

Animal Enclosures

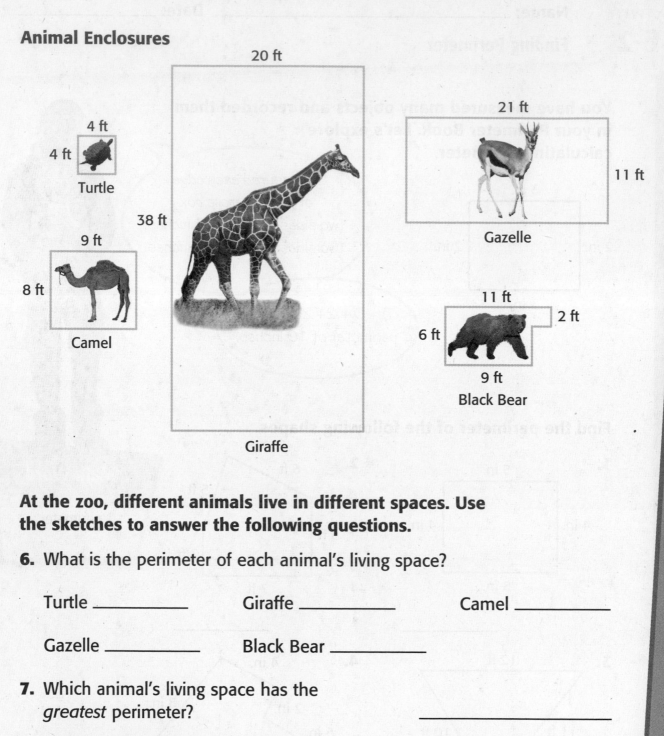

20 ft

4 ft

4 ft Turtle

38 ft

9 ft

8 ft Camel

Giraffe

21 ft

11 ft

Gazelle

11 ft

6 ft **2 ft**

9 ft

Black Bear

At the zoo, different animals live in different spaces. Use the sketches to answer the following questions.

6. What is the perimeter of each animal's living space?

Turtle _____   Giraffe _____   Camel _____

Gazelle _____   Black Bear _____

7. Which animal's living space has the *greatest* perimeter?   _____

8. Which animal's living space has the *least* perimeter?   _____

9. Which animal's living space has a perimeter about half as long as the camel's space?   _____

Draw a rectangle that could be filled with the given number of squares. Label the sides and write the area inside your drawing.

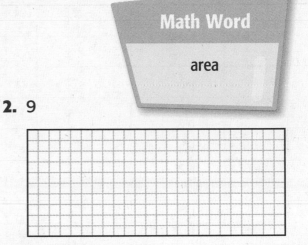

Math Word

area

1. 16

2. 9

3. 24

4. 17

5. Using Exercise 3, find at least one different rectangle with the same area. Can you find others? How many different rectangles can you find?

At Home

Compare the area of a bedroom door to the area of the top of a bed. Use the measuring tape you made in E-1, and round measurements to the nearest inch or centimeter. Which object has the smaller area?

Below is the floor plan for the new library at Hillside Elementary. The total available space for furniture is 272 square feet.

Hillside Elementary Library

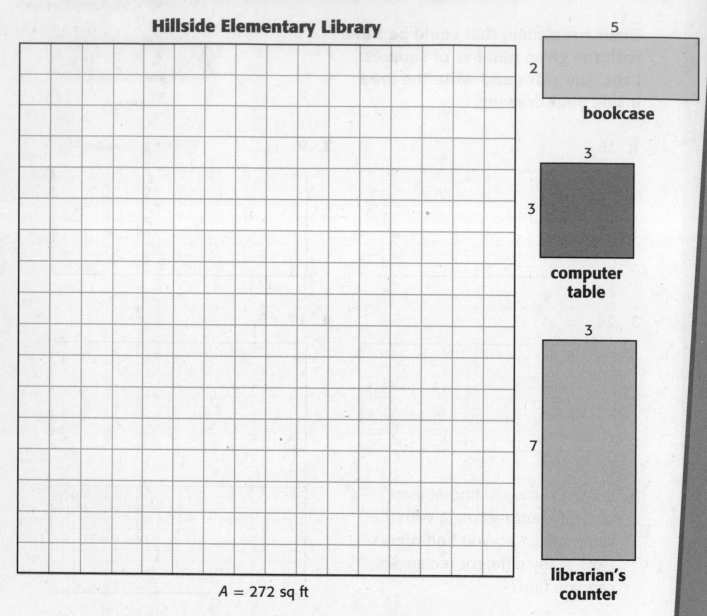

A = 272 sq ft

bookcase — 5 × 2

computer table — 3 × 3

librarian's counter — 3 × 7

6. If plans call for 12 bookcases, 5 computer tables, and 1 counter, is there enough floor space left for a 25 sq ft reading rug? Use the grid design above to draw your version of the library's floor plan. Let 1 cm² = 1 ft².

Relationships Between Perimeter and Area

You have calculated both perimeter and area of rectangles. Now let's see what happens to a rectangle's area when the perimeter stays the same.

For this activity, 7 × 3 will be the same as 3 × 7.

I can look at my data to see if I can find a relationship, or pattern.

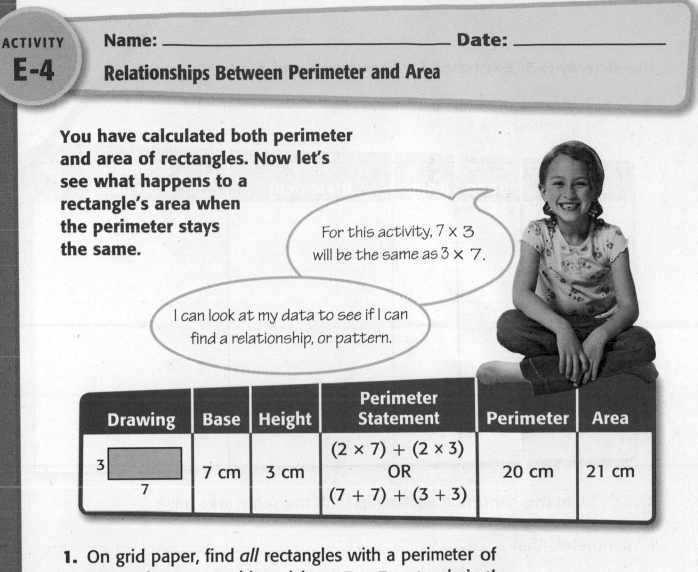

Drawing	Base	Height	Perimeter Statement	Perimeter	Area
3 ⬜ 7	7 cm	3 cm	(2 × 7) + (2 × 3) OR (7 + 7) + (3 + 3)	20 cm	21 cm

1. On grid paper, find *all* rectangles with a perimeter of 20 centimeters. In this activity, a 7 × 3 rectangle is the same as a 3 × 7. Only show one of those in your work.

2. Next, find the area of each rectangle you drew. Organize your work in a table, going from *greatest* area to *least* area.

Drawing	Base	Height	Perimeter Statement	Perimeter	Area

Use Activity E-3, Exercise 5 for Exercises 3 and 4.

3. Organize your findings in a table from the *least* perimeter to the *greatest*.

Drawing	Base	Height	Area Statement	Perimeter Statement

4. Complete this sentence: Rectangles with the same area have

perimeters that _____.

On grid paper, draw at least two rectangles with the given area.

5. 14 square units

6. 25 square units

7. 13 square units

8. 36 square units

PROJECT

In Feet

Use construction paper or other materials to create a square inch and a square foot. How many square inches are in a square foot?

Reflecting on What I Learned

New *Vocabulary* I learned:

1. _____

2. _____

3. _____

What are two key items I learned in this unit? _____

_____

_____

_____

List one relationship between perimeter and area that you have learned.

_____

_____

_____

Outside Your Classroom

Where will you see perimeter, area, and measurement outside the classroom?

- What would you think about when creating a tree house? Explain.

- What if you charged to rake leaves based on the perimeter of a yard or the area of a yard? When would you choose perimeter? area?

Designing an Outside Space

In this unit, you made rulers, measured perimeters and estimated the perimeters of different objects.

Use this new knowledge to design an outdoor area. This can be a garden, a playground area (with equipment) or your dream yard.

1. Use 50 color tiles to plan your outside space. Explore different shapes and sizes.

   - Think about where objects would go.

   - What shape will work best for your space?

   - Write the questions you considered when exploring your design.

   - How will you use the math in this unit during your project?

2. Cut a piece of grid paper the same size and shape as your space. Clearly label the parts of your space. Make sure to label all edges with the correct measurements.

3. Write a report on your project including some of the following.

   - What kind of space did you design?

   - How big is it? How will the area be used? What items did you put into your space?

   - What measurements can you include?

   - You may even want to include a picture with color.

UNIT F

Congruence and Symmetry

In this unit, I will:

- Identify and draw congruent figures
- Slide, turn, and flip figures
- Draw lines of symmetry

Review Concepts
- figure, pattern

Projects
- Symmetry Mobile
- Designing a Symmetrical Building

Game
- Congruent Match-Up

New Vocabulary

congruent   two figures having the same size and the same shape

flip (reflection)   move a figure across a line to create a mirror image of the figure

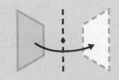

line of symmetry   a line on which a figure can be folded so that its two halves match exactly

similar   two figures that have the same shape but are not the same size

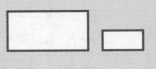

slide (translation)   move a figure in a vertical, horizontal, or diagonal direction

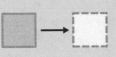

turn (rotation)   move a figure around a point

Home Letter

English
English

During this math unit, your student will be exploring congruent figures and symmetry. To help with learning, here are some activities to do at home.

- Find objects that are the same shape and size.
- Draw half of a shape and have your student complete the shape to make a figure with symmetry.
- Flip, turn, or slide objects with your student.

In class, your student will be:

- using models to create congruent and symmetrical figures;
- classifying figures as congruent or similar and identifying positions as a slide, turn, or flip.

Español

Durante esta unidad de matemáticas, su estudiante va a explorar las figuras congruentes y la simetría. Para ayudar con el aprendizaje, sugerimos estas actividades para hacer en casa:

- Encuentre objetos que tengan la misma forma y tamaño.
- Dibuje la mitad de una forma y pídale a su estudiante que la complete para hacer una figura con simetría.
- Voltee, gire o deslice objetos con su estudiante.

En clase, su estudiante va a:

- usar modelos para crear figuras congruentes y simétricas;
- clasificar figuras como congruentes y similares e identificar posiciones como un deslizamiento, un giro o una vuelta.

Name: _____ Date: _____

Congruent Figures

In the investigation, you explored similar and congruent figures.

Draw a congruent figure.

1.

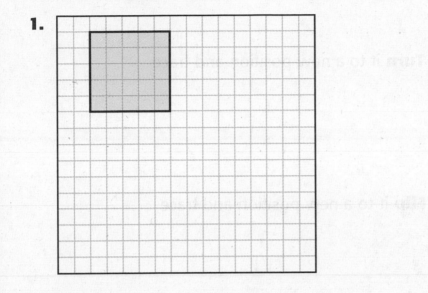

Math Words

congruent

flip

similar

slide

turn

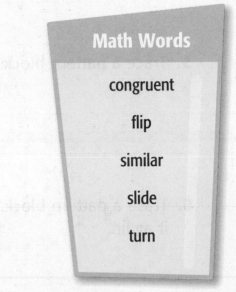

2.

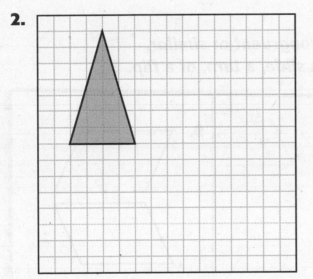

3.

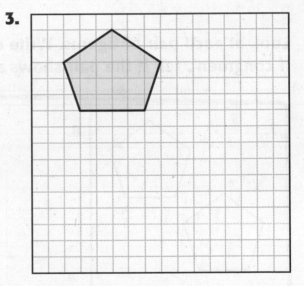

At Home

Look around your home. Make a list of things that are congruent.

You can move a figure and its size and shape stay the same.

4. Trace a pattern block. **Slide** it to a new position and trace it again.

5. Trace a pattern block. **Turn** it to a new position and trace it again.

6. Trace a pattern block. **Flip** it to a new position and trace it again.

Look at each pair of figures. Write *congruent* or *similar*. If congruent, tell if the pair shows a *slide*, a *turn*, or a *flip*.

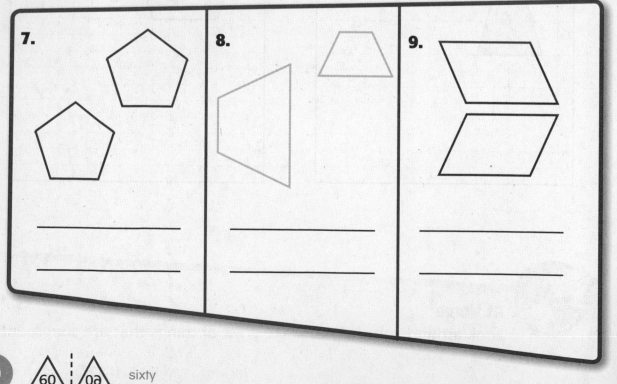

7.

8.

9.

In the investigation, you identified figures that have symmetry. Some figures will have more than one line of symmetry.

1. Make a square on your geoboard using rubber bands.

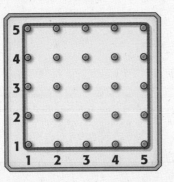

2. Make a line of symmetry with a rubber band.

3. Turn the board. Make another line of symmetry.

4. How many lines of symmetry can you make? _____

Draw your square and the lines of symmetry below.

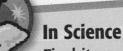

In Science
Find items in nature that have symmetry. Make a symmetry poster. Draw pictures, find photographs, display the actual item, or cut out pictures in magazines. Label your discoveries.

Draw the lines of symmetry for each figure.

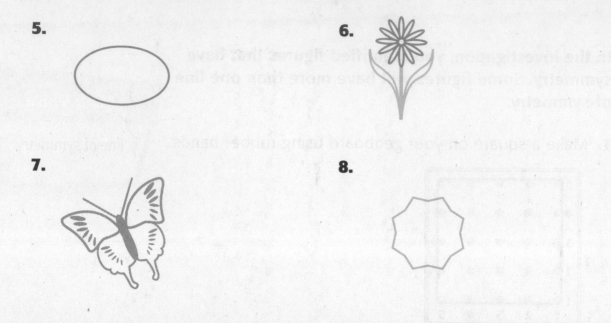

5.

6.

7.

8.

Look at each figure. Write *yes* if it has a line of symmetry. Draw one line of symmetry. Write *no* if it does not.

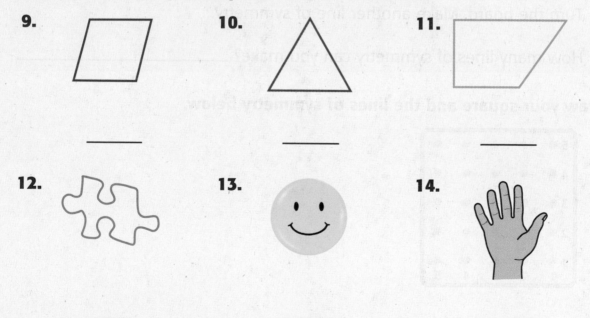

9.

10.

11.

_____

_____

12.

13.

14.

_____

_____

_____

Which uppercase alphabet letters have symmetry?

15. Write five letters and draw their lines of symmetry.

Name: _____ **Date:** _____

Creating Figures with Symmetry

Draw figures that have symmetry.

1. Shade in more squares to make a figure with symmetry.

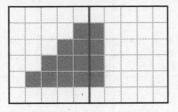

Draw the matching part to make a figure with symmetry.

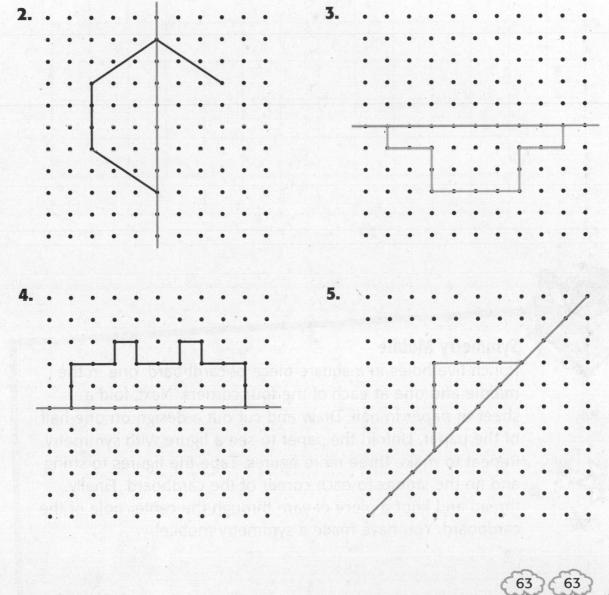

2.

3.

4.

5.

6. Draw your own design with symmetry. You may create it first with pattern blocks. Then draw it on the grid below.

Symmetry Mobile

Punch five holes in a square piece of cardboard, one in the middle and one at each of the four corners. Next, fold a sheet of paper in half. Draw and cut out a design on one-half of the paper. Unfold the paper to see a figure with symmetry. Repeat to make three more figures. Tape the figures to string and tie the strings to each corner of the cardboard. Finally, thread and knot a piece of yarn through the center hole of the cardboard. You have made a symmetry mobile!

Reflecting on What I Learned

New *Vocabulary* I learned:

1. _____

_____

2. _____

_____

3. _____

Can a figure have more than 1 line of symmetry? Explain.

_____

_____

What is the difference between congruent figures and similar figures?

_____

Outside Your Classroom

Where will you see congruent figures and symmetry outside the classroom?

- Does your home have a line of symmetry? Does it have congruent parts?

- Does a car have a line of symmetry?

- Does a dog's face have symmetry? Why or why not?

Design a Symmetrical Building

Create a model of a building using geometric solids. Then draw a plan of the building.

1. Use geometric solids to design a model of a building. Your building should have symmetry.

   - Is your building a house, an apartment building, or a skyscraper?

   - What shape and size is your building?

   - Does your building have symmetry? Where is the line of symmetry?

2. Next, draw a plan of your building.

   - How will you draw the building? Will you draw it in parts or as a whole?

   - What figures will you use to make your building?

   - How large is your building?

3. Finally, write a report that tells about your building and how you designed it.

   - What is your building? Include the drawing plan.

   - What figures did you use to design it? Did you turn, slide, or flip congruent figures to make your design?

   - What challenges did you have drawing the plan?

UNIT G

Understanding Fractions

In this unit, I will:

- Use pattern blocks to represent fractions
- Create a fraction kit
- Add fractions to find names for 1 whole
- Relate fractions to money

Review Concepts
- geometric shapes
- coin values

Projects
- What's In My Desk?
- Make a Fraction Book

Game
- Basketball Fractions

New Vocabulary

denominator the part of the fraction that tells how many equal parts the whole is broken into

In $\frac{5}{6}$, 6 is the denominator.

fraction a number that represents part of a whole or part of a set

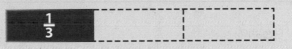

hexagon a polygon with six sides and six angles

numerator the part of the fraction that tells how many of the equal parts are being used

In $\frac{5}{6}$, 5 is the numerator.

trapezoid a four-sided shape with only two opposite sides that are the same length

triangle a polygon with three sides and three angles

Home Letter

Copyright © Macmillan/McGraw-Hill, a division of The McGraw-Hill Companies, Inc.

English

During this math unit, your student will be learning fraction concepts. To help with learning, here are things to do at home.

- Find fractional parts using foods, such as eggs from an egg carton or partially used packs of juice boxes.
- Use measuring tools when cooking and invite your student to measure with you.
- Count coin collections and express the value as fractional parts of a dollar.
- Discuss time in terms of fractions of an hour.

Español

Durante esta unidad de matemáticas, su estudiante va a aprender conceptos de fracciones. Para ayudar con el aprendizaje, sugerimos estas actividades para hacer en casa:

- Encuentre partes fraccionarias usando alimentos, tales como los huevos de un cartón de huevos o los empaques parcialmente usados de cajitas de jugo.
- Use las herramientas de medición cuando esté cocinando e invite a su estudiante a medir con usted.
- Cuente colecciones de monedas y exprese el valor como partes fraccionarias de un dólar.
- Comente la hora en términos de fracciones de hora.

Pattern Block Fractions

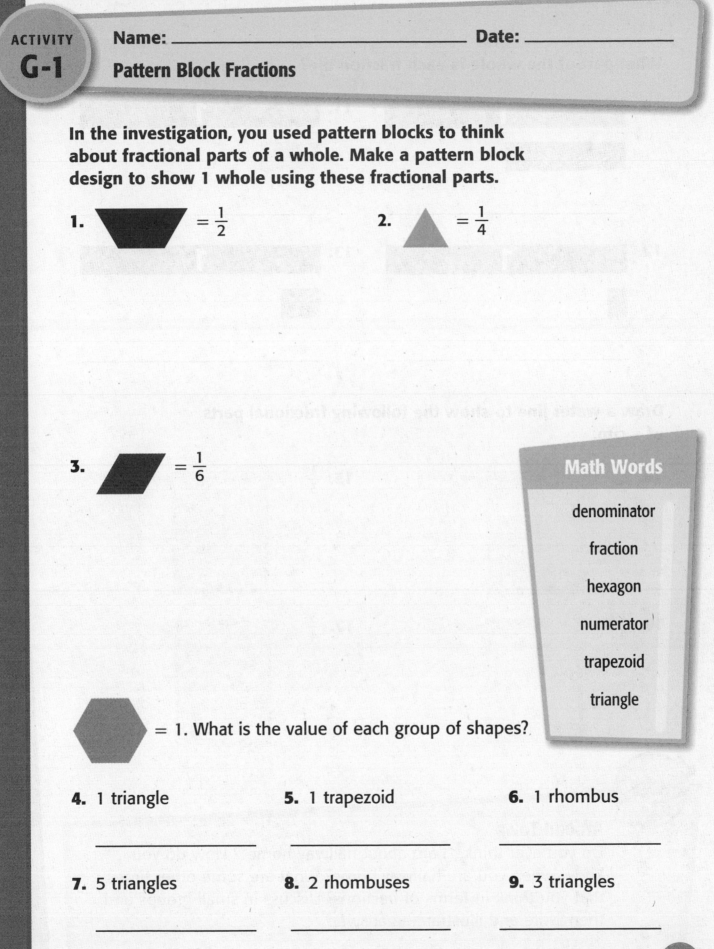

In the investigation, you used pattern blocks to think about fractional parts of a whole. Make a pattern block design to show 1 whole using these fractional parts.

1. $= \frac{1}{2}$

2. $= \frac{1}{4}$

3. $= \frac{1}{6}$

Math Words

denominator

fraction

hexagon

numerator

trapezoid

triangle

= 1. What is the value of each group of shapes?

4. 1 triangle

5. 1 trapezoid

6. 1 rhombus

_____   _____   _____

7. 5 triangles

8. 2 rhombuses

9. 3 triangles

_____   _____   _____

What part of the whole is each fraction tile?

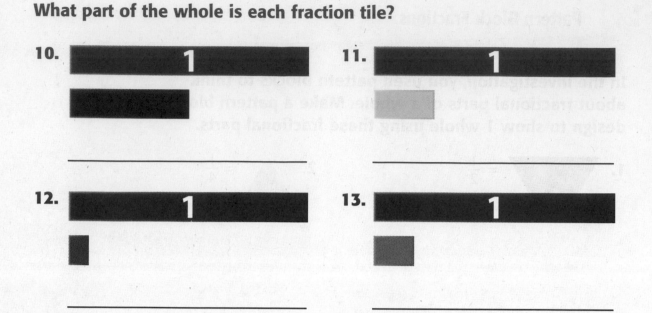

10. **1**

_____

11. **1**

_____

12. **1**

_____

13. **1**

_____

Draw a water line to show the following fractional parts of a cup.

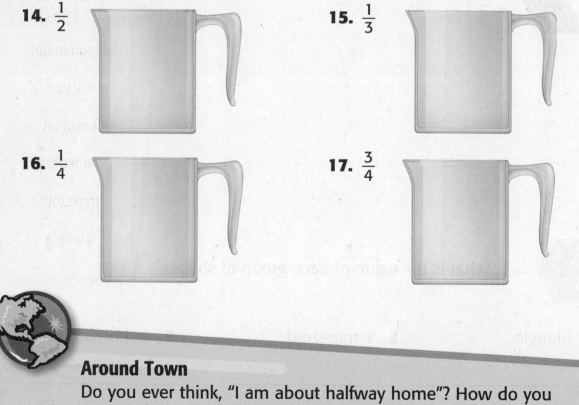

14. $\frac{1}{2}$

15. $\frac{1}{3}$

16. $\frac{1}{4}$

17. $\frac{3}{4}$

Around Town

Do you ever think, "I am about halfway home"? How do you know when you are halfway home? What are some other times that you think in terms of fractions? Discuss in small groups and then write and illustrate an answer.

Name: _____ Date: _____

Fractions and Wholes

In the investigation, you made your own fraction kit. Use your kit and reasoning skills to find the following.

How many of each piece do you need to make 1 whole?
Write the number as a fraction.

1. eighths _____   2. thirds _____   3. sixths _____

4. halves _____   5. twelfths _____   6. fourths _____

Complete. Use your fraction kit to help.

7.

$\frac{1}{4}$ and _____ make 1 whole.

$\frac{1}{4}$ + _____ = 1

8.

$\frac{2}{3}$ and _____ make 1 whole.

$\frac{2}{3}$ + _____ = 1

9.

$\frac{3}{6}$ and _____ make 1 whole.

$\frac{3}{6}$ + _____ = 1

10.

$\frac{3}{8}$ and _____ make 1 whole.

$\frac{3}{8}$ + _____ = 1

11.

$\frac{7}{12}$ and _____ make 1 whole.

$\frac{7}{12}$ + _____ = 1

12.

$\frac{1}{2}$ and _____ make 1 whole.

$\frac{1}{2}$ + _____ = 1

Write the fraction shown. What fractional part is missing?

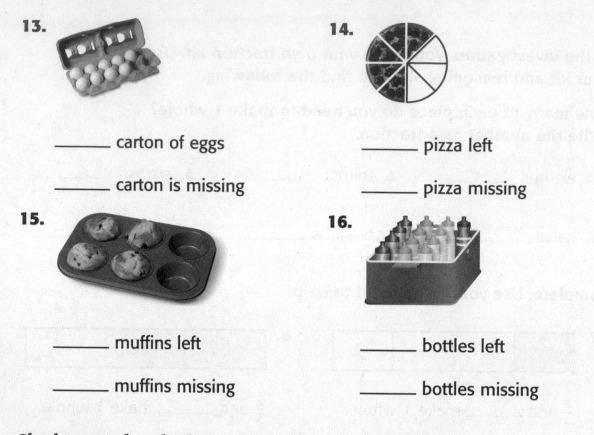

13.

_____ carton of eggs

_____ carton is missing

14.

_____ pizza left

_____ pizza missing

15.

_____ muffins left

_____ muffins missing

16.

_____ bottles left

_____ bottles missing

Shade part of each pie to show it is eaten. Tell the part that is eaten and the part that is left.

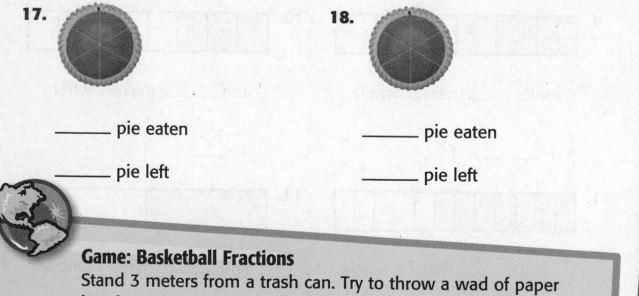

17.

_____ pie eaten

_____ pie left

18.

_____ pie eaten

_____ pie left

Game: Basketball Fractions

Stand 3 meters from a trash can. Try to throw a wad of paper into it 10 times. How many times did you get the paper into the basket? How many times did you miss? Write fractions to show your answers. Add the fractions. What is their sum?

Name: _____   Date: _____

Fractions and Money

In the investigation, you learned that coins are fractions of a dollar. Fractions can help you solve problems with money.

$1 for 10 Stickers

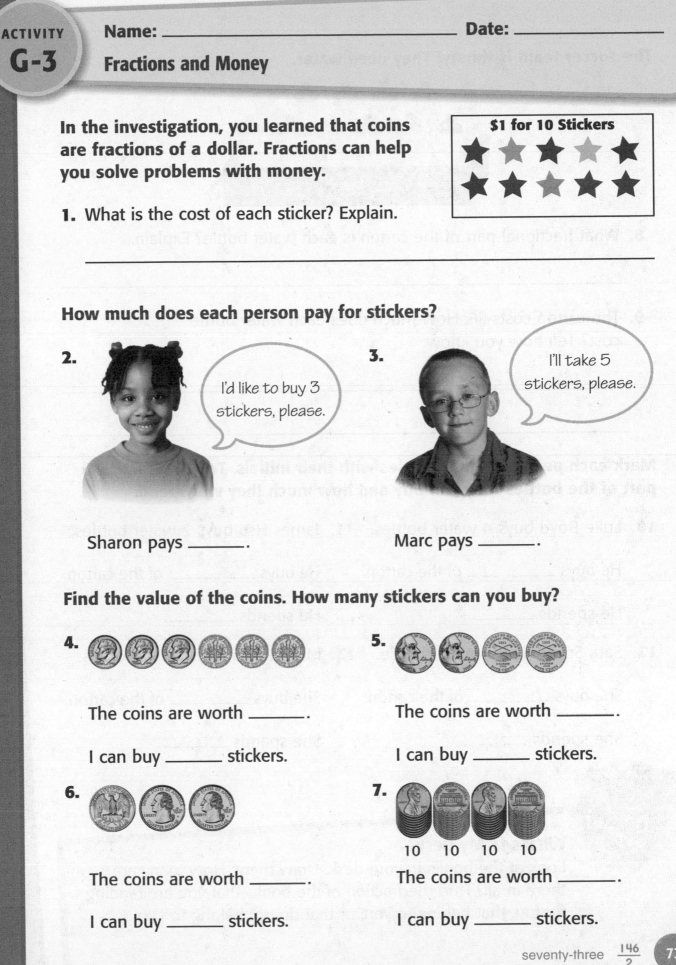

1. What is the cost of each sticker? Explain.

_____

How much does each person pay for stickers?

2.

I'd like to buy 3 stickers, please.

3.

I'll take 5 stickers, please.

Sharon pays _____.

Marc pays _____.

Find the value of the coins. How many stickers can you buy?

4.

The coins are worth _____.

I can buy _____ stickers.

5.

The coins are worth _____.

I can buy _____ stickers.

6.

The coins are worth _____.

I can buy _____ stickers.

7.

10   10   10   10

The coins are worth _____.

I can buy _____ stickers.

The soccer team is thirsty! They need water.

8. What fractional part of the carton is each water bottle? Explain.

_____

9. The carton costs $6. How much does each water bottle cost? Tell how you know.

_____

_____

Mark each person's water bottles with their initials. Tell the fractional part of the bottles they will buy and how much they will spend.

10. Luke Boyd buys 4 water bottles.

He buys _____ of the carton.

He spends _____.

11. James Hsu buys 2 water bottles.

He buys _____ of the carton.

He spends _____.

12. Sara Smith buys 1 water bottle.

She buys _____ of the carton.

She spends _____.

13. Mary May buys 5 water bottles.

She buys _____ of the carton.

She spends _____.

What's In My Desk?

Look at the books in your desk. Draw them. How many are there in all? Find the fraction of the books that you are reading for fun, that belong to you, or that do not belong to you.

Reflecting on What I Learned

New *Vocabulary* I learned:

1. _____

   _____

2. _____

   _____

What did I learn about fractions in this unit?

_____

_____

Describe one relationship between money and fractions.

_____

_____

_____

Outside Your Classroom

Where will you use fractions outside the classroom? How can you use fractions to:

- make a new recipe or craft project?
- find lengths or distances?
- find the cost per unit of food, drink, or toys?

Make a Fraction Book

In this unit, you made a fraction kit and related fractions to measurement and money. Now create a fraction book.

1. First, think about all the ways you can show $\frac{1}{2}$. Explore different applications of $\frac{1}{2}$. Think about:

   - $\frac{1}{2}$ of a shape. How many ways can you fold a square piece of paper to show $\frac{1}{2}$?

   - $\frac{1}{2}$ of a group. What is the relationship between $\frac{1}{2}$ of the group and the whole group?

   - How many ways can you show money amounts equivalent to $\frac{1}{2}$ of $1?

   - What are some other ways you can show $\frac{1}{2}$ in measurement or in hours or days?

2. Show $\frac{1}{2}$ in as many different ways as you can. Fold and draw lines on the construction paper shapes. Draw pictures of other ways. Label and display all of the ways on manila paper.

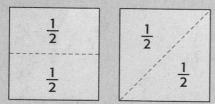

3. Repeat Steps 1 and 2 for other fractions such as $\frac{1}{4}$, $\frac{3}{4}$, and $\frac{1}{8}$.

4. Write an introduction to your fraction book. Tell how you completed your project and explain your thinking. Staple the pages together to complete your fraction book.

UNIT H

Comparing Fractions

In this unit, I will:

- Find equivalent fractions
- Learn and understand rules for comparing fractions
- Apply fractions to money and other real-life applications

Review Concepts
- meaning of fractions
- fractional parts of a whole
- adding/subtracting fractions with like denominators

Projects
- Equivalent Fraction Posters
- Make a Fraction Web

Games
- Comparison Concentration
- What's the Deal?

New Vocabulary

benchmark   a number used as a guide for making an estimate

equivalent fractions   fractions that have the same value

$$\frac{2}{4} = \frac{1}{2}$$

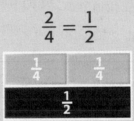

estimate   a number close to an exact value; an estimate indicates *about* how much

$$47 + 22 \text{ is about } 70$$

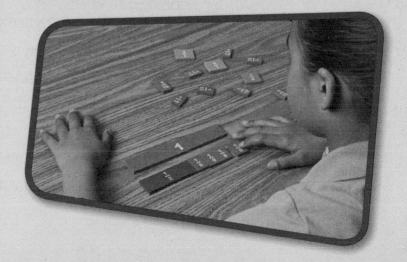

Home Letter

English

During this math unit, your student will be finding equivalent fractions and comparing and ordering fractions. To help with learning, here are things to do at home.

- Use pizza, egg cartons, and other multi-item packages to express equivalent fractions. For example, 6 eggs in a 12-egg carton is $\frac{1}{2}$ carton or $\frac{6}{12}$ eggs.
- Compare fractional parts of ingredients in a recipe.
- Toss 15 pennies on the floor or table. Have your student write a fraction for the amount of pennies that lands heads-up.

In class, your student will be:

- using fraction pieces to model equivalence;
- using rules to compare and order fractions;
- making a fraction web.

Español

Durante esta unidad de matemáticas, su estudiante va a encontrar fracciones equivalentes y comparar y ordenar fracciones. Para ayudar con el aprendizaje, sugerimos estas actividades para hacer en casa:

- Use pizza, cartones de huevos y otros empaques de múltiples artículos para expresar fracciones equivalentes. Por ejemplo, 6 huevos en un cartón de una docena son $\frac{1}{2}$ cartón o $\frac{6}{12}$ huevos.
- Compare partes fraccionarias de ingredientes en una receta.
- Lance 15 monedas de un centavo al piso o a una mesa. Pídale a su estudiante que escriba una fracción para la cantidad de monedas que cayeron cara arriba.

En clase su estudiante va a:

- usar piezas de fracciones para dar ejemplos de equivalencia;
- usar las reglas para comparar y ordenar fracciones;
- hacer una red de fracciones.

Name: _____ Date: _____

Equivalent Fractions

Calculate equivalent fractions.

Maria, Billy, and Suzi are sharing a box of 3 popsicles.

1. Circle Billy's popsicle. What fraction of the box did you circle?

   _____

   Maria   Billy   Suzi

They decide to eat $\frac{1}{2}$ now and $\frac{1}{2}$ later.

2. How many pieces are there now?

   _____ pieces

3. What fraction of the 6 pieces did Billy eat altogether? _____

Draw lines and write equivalent fractions.

4. Draw a line to show eighths.

   $\frac{1}{4} = \frac{}{8}$

5. Draw lines to show sixths.

   $\frac{1}{2} = \frac{}{6}$

6. Draw lines to show ninths.

   $\frac{1}{3} = \frac{}{9}$

7. Draw lines to show twelfths.

   $\frac{1}{3} = \frac{}{12}$

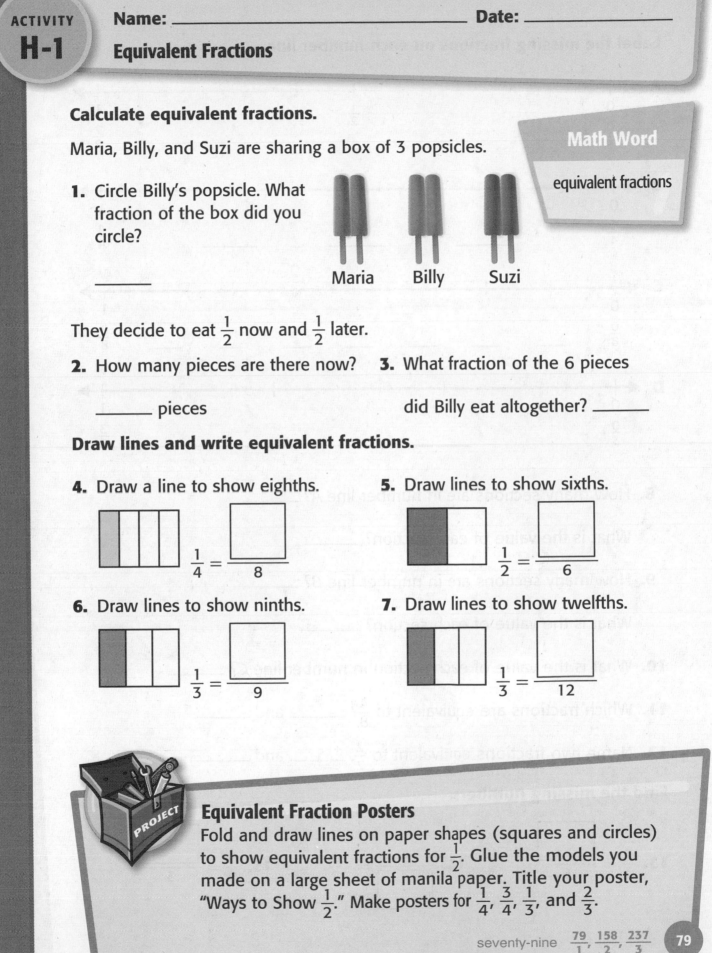

Equivalent Fraction Posters

Fold and draw lines on paper shapes (squares and circles) to show equivalent fractions for $\frac{1}{2}$. Glue the models you made on a large sheet of manila paper. Title your poster, "Ways to Show $\frac{1}{2}$." Make posters for $\frac{1}{4}$, $\frac{3}{4}$, $\frac{1}{3}$, and $\frac{2}{3}$.

Label the missing fractions on each number line.

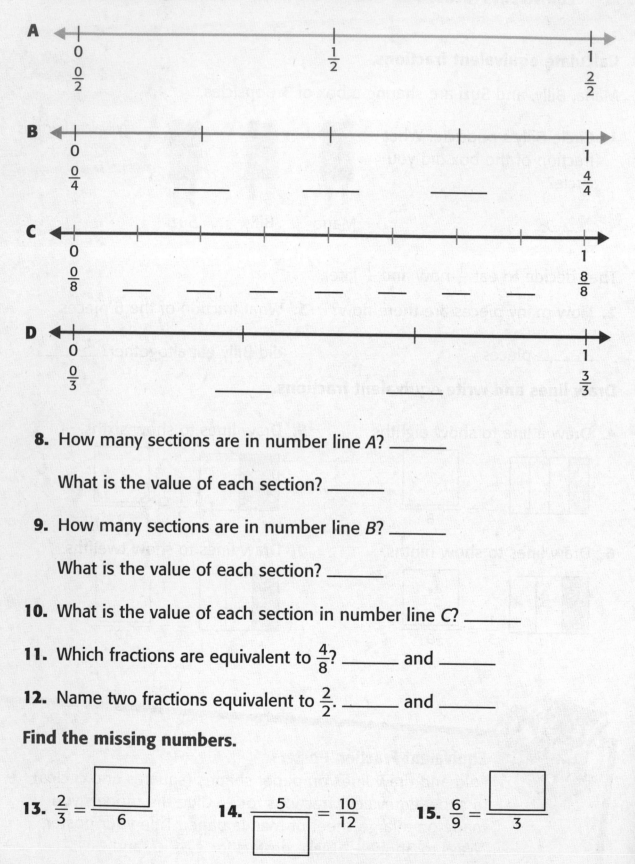

8. How many sections are in number line *A*? _____

What is the value of each section? _____

9. How many sections are in number line *B*? _____

What is the value of each section? _____

10. What is the value of each section in number line *C*? _____

11. Which fractions are equivalent to $\frac{4}{8}$? _____ and _____

12. Name two fractions equivalent to $\frac{2}{2}$. _____ and _____

Find the missing numbers.

13. $\frac{2}{3} = \frac{\boxed{}}{6}$

14. $\frac{5}{\boxed{}} = \frac{10}{12}$

15. $\frac{6}{9} = \frac{\boxed{}}{3}$

Name: _____ Date: _____

Constructing Rules to Compare Fractions

In the investigation, you constructed rules to compare fractions. Put your rules to the test!

> When the **denominators** are the same, the fraction with the *greater numerator* has the greater value.

> When the **numerators** are the same, the fraction with the *lesser denominator* has the greater value.

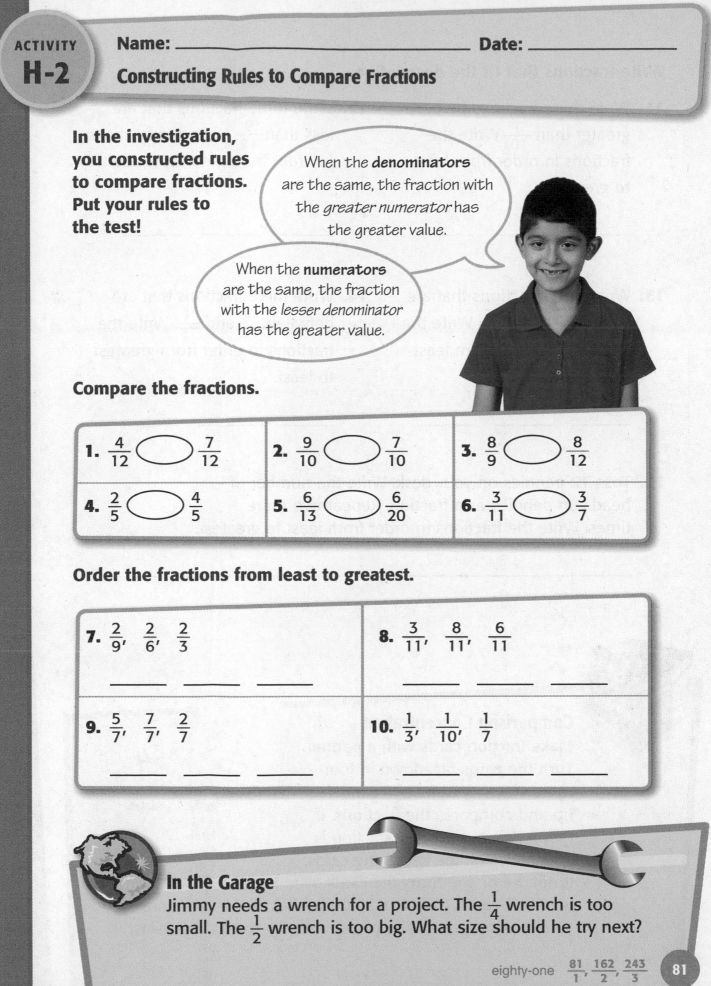

Compare the fractions.

1. $\frac{4}{12}$ ◯ $\frac{7}{12}$

2. $\frac{9}{10}$ ◯ $\frac{7}{10}$

3. $\frac{8}{9}$ ◯ $\frac{8}{12}$

4. $\frac{2}{5}$ ◯ $\frac{4}{5}$

5. $\frac{6}{13}$ ◯ $\frac{6}{20}$

6. $\frac{3}{11}$ ◯ $\frac{3}{7}$

Order the fractions from least to greatest.

7. $\frac{2}{9}$, $\frac{2}{6}$, $\frac{2}{3}$

____ ____ ____

8. $\frac{3}{11}$, $\frac{8}{11}$, $\frac{6}{11}$

____ ____ ____

9. $\frac{5}{7}$, $\frac{7}{7}$, $\frac{2}{7}$

____ ____ ____

10. $\frac{1}{3}$, $\frac{1}{10}$, $\frac{1}{7}$

____ ____ ____

In the Garage

Jimmy needs a wrench for a project. The $\frac{1}{4}$ wrench is too small. The $\frac{1}{2}$ wrench is too big. What size should he try next?

Write fractions that fit the description.

11. Write three fractions that are greater than $\frac{1}{10}$. Write the fractions in order from least to greatest.

_____ , _____ , _____

12. Write three fractions that are less than $\frac{9}{12}$. Write the fractions in order from greatest to least.

_____ , _____ , _____

13. Write three fractions that are between $\frac{3}{20}$ and $\frac{3}{4}$. Write the fractions in order from least to greatest.

_____ , _____ , _____

14. Write three fractions that are between $\frac{12}{15}$ and $\frac{4}{15}$. Write the fractions in order from greatest to least.

_____ , _____ , _____

15. Toss 12 pennies on your desk. Write the number of heads-up pennies as a fraction. Repeat two more times. Write the fractions in order from least to greatest.

_____

Comparison Concentration

Make fraction cards with a partner. Turn the cards facedown in four rows. Player A turns two cards face up and compares the fractions. If Player A can say which fraction is greater, he or she keeps the cards. If not, he or she turns the cards over. Player B repeats with two new cards. Players take turns until all the cards are correctly compared. The player with the most cards wins.

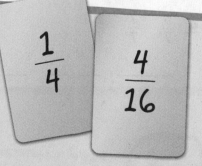

Name: _____   Date: _____

More About Comparing Fractions

In the investigation, you used estimation and
equivalence to compare fractions. Use these
strategies to compare and order more fractions.

Math Words

benchmark

estimate

1. Classify each fraction as close to 0, $\frac{1}{2}$, or 1.
   Write them in the table below.

$\frac{1}{20}$ $\frac{7}{16}$ $\frac{1}{12}$ $\frac{5}{8}$ $\frac{19}{20}$ $\frac{14}{16}$ $\frac{11}{20}$ $\frac{2}{16}$ $\frac{11}{12}$ $\frac{1}{8}$ $\frac{5}{12}$ $\frac{17}{20}$

About 0	About $\frac{1}{2}$	About 1

Use the information in the table to order the fractions
from least to greatest.

2. $\frac{5}{12}$, $\frac{17}{20}$, $\frac{2}{16}$

_____ _____ _____

3. $\frac{11}{12}$, $\frac{1}{8}$, $\frac{7}{16}$

_____ _____ _____

4. $\frac{1}{20}$, $\frac{14}{16}$, $\frac{5}{8}$

_____ _____ _____

5. $\frac{19}{20}$, $\frac{1}{12}$, $\frac{11}{20}$

_____ _____ _____

6. $\frac{3}{4}$ _____ $\frac{7}{8}$

7. $\frac{2}{7}$ _____ $\frac{5}{14}$

8. $\frac{6}{10}$ _____ $\frac{1}{2}$

9. $\frac{1}{3}$ _____ $\frac{2}{9}$

10. $\frac{3}{12}$ _____ $\frac{1}{4}$

11. $\frac{15}{20}$ _____ $\frac{4}{5}$

Write the fractions in order on the number line.

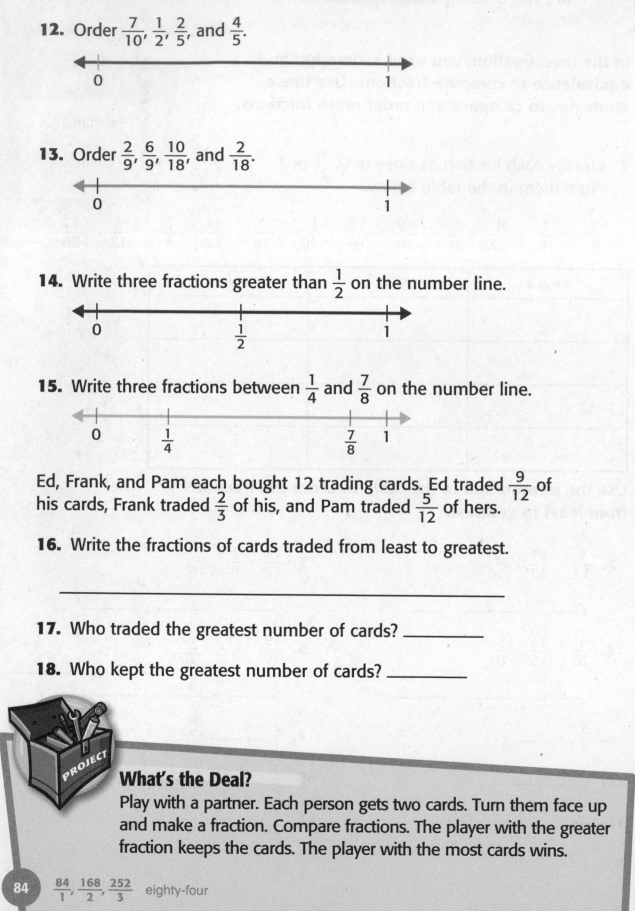

12. Order $\frac{7}{10}$, $\frac{1}{2}$, $\frac{2}{5}$, and $\frac{4}{5}$.

0 ————————————— 1

13. Order $\frac{2}{9}$, $\frac{6}{9}$, $\frac{10}{18}$, and $\frac{2}{18}$.

0 ————————————— 1

14. Write three fractions greater than $\frac{1}{2}$ on the number line.

0 ———— $\frac{1}{2}$ ———— 1

15. Write three fractions between $\frac{1}{4}$ and $\frac{7}{8}$ on the number line.

0 —— $\frac{1}{4}$ ———— $\frac{7}{8}$ — 1

Ed, Frank, and Pam each bought 12 trading cards. Ed traded $\frac{9}{12}$ of his cards, Frank traded $\frac{2}{3}$ of his, and Pam traded $\frac{5}{12}$ of hers.

16. Write the fractions of cards traded from least to greatest.

_____

17. Who traded the greatest number of cards? _____

18. Who kept the greatest number of cards? _____

PROJECT

What's the Deal?
Play with a partner. Each person gets two cards. Turn them face up and make a fraction. Compare fractions. The player with the greater fraction keeps the cards. The player with the most cards wins.

Reflecting on What I Learned

New *Vocabulary* I learned:

1. _____

2. _____

What are some ways to find equivalent fractions?

_____

_____

What are some strategies I can use to compare fractions?

_____

_____

_____

_____

Outside Your Classroom

Where do you see fractions outside the classroom?

- Ingredients listed in a recipe?

- In sports?

- With tools?

Fruit Salad

$\frac{1}{4}$ cup blueberries

$\frac{1}{2}$ cup strawberries

$\frac{3}{4}$ cup grapes

4 bananas sliced

3 apples sliced

Mix together in a large bowl.

Make a Fraction Web

Use your knowledge of fractions to create a fraction web.

1. Choose a fraction with a *denominator* between 3 and 10.

2. Create a web showing your fractions.

   - Show your fraction with pictures and on a number line.

   - Find two fractions equivalent to your fraction. Find fractions that are greater than and less than your fraction.

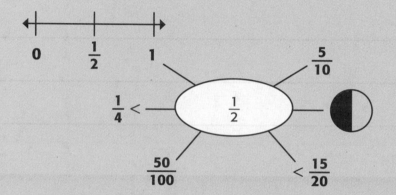

3. Beneath your web, show your fraction in a comparison chart. Fill in at least 5 rows of the chart.

$\frac{1}{2}$		
<	=	>
$\frac{1}{4}$	$\frac{5}{10}$	$\frac{15}{20}$

4. Write a report on your project including some of the following: How did you find equivalences for your fraction web? What strategies did you use to identify fractions greater than and less than your fraction?

UNIT 1

Estimating and Measuring Lengths

In this unit, I will:

- Make measuring tools
- Estimate, measure, and compare lengths
- Measure using inches, feet, and yards
- Measure using centimeters, decimeters, and meters

Review Concept
- perimeter

Projects
- Handy Units
- Designing a Game

New Vocabulary

centimeter (cm) a metric unit for measuring length and height

100 centimeters = 1 meter

customary system the measurement system that includes units such as foot, pound, quart, and degrees Fahrenheit; also called standard measurement

decimeter (dm) a metric unit for measuring length and height

1 decimeter = 10 centimeters

meter (m) a metric unit for measuring length

1 meter = 100 centimeters

metric system the measurement system based on powers of 10 that includes units such as meter, gram, and liter

yard (yd) a customary unit for measuring length

1 yard = 3 feet or 36 inches

Home Letter

English

During this math unit, your student will be exploring measuring tools. To help with learning, here are things to do at home.

- Estimate and compare lengths of objects. For example, "Will the cereal box height fit on this pantry shelf?"

- Measure objects using nonstandard units, such as pennies, and standard units, such as inches.

- Play games describing the length of an object and have your student name the object. For example, "I am longer than one foot, but shorter than 2 feet. I am black. What am I?" *computer keyboard*

In class, your student will be:

- making measuring tools and estimating, measuring, and comparing lengths.

Español

Durante esta unidad de matemáticas, su estudiante va a explorar la medición por medio. Para ayudar con el aprendizaje, sugerimos estas actividades para hacer en casa:

- Calcule las longitudes de algunos objetos y compárelas. Por ejemplo, "¿Cabrá una caja de cereal de esta altura en la repisa de alacena?"

- Mida objetos con unidades no estándares, tales como monedas de un centavo, y también con unidades estándar, como pulgadas.

- Juegue a describir la longitud de un objeto y pídale a su estudiante que diga el nombre del objeto. Por ejemplo, "Mido más de un pie, pero menos de dos. Soy de color negro. ¿Qué soy?" *El teclado de la computadora.*

En clase, su estudiante va a:

- crear herramientas de medición y hacer estimaciones, medir y comparar longitudes.

Name: _____ Date: _____

Measuring with Nonstandard Units

Compare the length of Path A from the investigation to other items in the classroom.

1. List at least three things for each category.

Shorter than Path A	About the same as Path A	Longer than Path A

Find these objects in your classroom. Measure each object using cubes.

2. pencil   **3.** crayon box   **4.** math book

about _____ cubes   about _____ cubes   about _____ cubes

Handy Units

Measure different objects around your classroom. Use your hand as the unit of measurement. Estimate first, then measure. Create a table. Compare your measurements with other students' measurements.

Object	Measurement in Hand Spans
desk top	4

You can use different units to measure the same object.

5. About how many paper clips long is the string?

about _____ paper clips

6. About how many cubes long is the string?

about _____ cubes

7. Draw a line that is six cubes long.

8. Emma's necklace is 10 paper clips long. About how many cubes long is the necklace?

about _____ cubes

Find the perimeter of these objects.

9. your math book

Estimate: about _____ cubes

Measurement: about _____ cubes

10. your desk top

Estimate: about _____ large paper clips

Measurement: about _____ large paper clips

Name: _____ Date: _____

Measuring with Customary Units

In the investigation, you measured to the nearest $\frac{1}{2}$ inch.

The pencil is about
$3\frac{1}{2}$ inches long.

The board is about 9 feet
or 3 yards long.

Math Words

customary system

yard (yd)

Estimate and then use your tools to measure to the
nearest $\frac{1}{2}$ inch or foot. Circle the unit you used.

1. width of your hand

Estimate: about _____

Measurement: about _____

inches   feet

2. your height

Estimate: about _____

Measurement: about _____

inches   feet

3. your reach

Estimate: about _____

Measurement: about _____

inches   feet

4. length of your foot

Estimate: about _____

Measurement: about _____

inches   feet

You can also measure length in yards.

$$1 \text{ yard} = 3 \text{ feet} \qquad 1 \text{ yard} = 36 \text{ inches}$$

5. Compare the lengths to 1 yard. Name two things for each.

Shorter than 1 yd	About 1 yd	Longer than 1 yd

Complete the tables to solve the problems.

Adam's room is 4 yards long.

6. How many feet long is Adam's room?

Yards	1	2	3	4
Feet	3			

7. How many inches long is Adam's room?

Yards	1	2	3	4
Inches	36			

8. How many yards long is your measuring tape? _____

Explain how you solved this problem. _____

_____

_____

At Home
Measure the length of a jump for each person in your family.
Use chalk to mark the start of the jump and the end of the jump.
Estimate whose jump will be the longest and whose jump will be
the shortest. Compare your estimates with the measurements.

Name: _____ Date: _____

Measuring with Metric Units

You made metric measuring tools. Use these tools to help you list two objects that are about the given lengths below.

1. 1 centimeter _____

2. 1 decimeter _____

3. 1 meter _____

Estimate. Then measure to the nearest centimeter or meter.

4. length of your foot	Estimate: about _____ Measurement: about _____
5. length of one step	Estimate: about _____ Measurement: about _____

In Science

On the playground, stand in one place. Have a partner measure the length of your shadow. Repeat later in the day. How does the length of your shadow change? Why do you think the shadow length changes? How does the length of your shadow compare with your height?

Write the letter of the best estimate.

6. length of a nail	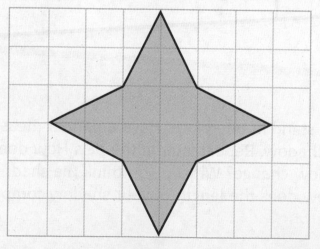	
7. length of a car		
8. width of a finger		
9. height of a tall adult man		

A. about 1 cm

B. about 2 m

C. about 4 m

D. about 4 cm

Write the lengths in order from least to greatest.

10. _____

11. Draw a rectangular frame to put around the star.
Write the length and width of the frame.

_____

_____

Reflecting on What I Learned

New *Vocabulary* I learned:

1. _____

2. _____

3. _____

List one relationship between centimeters, decimeters, and meters you learned.

_____

_____

List one relationship between inches, feet, and yards you learned.

_____

_____

Outside Your Classroom

Where will you see measurement of length outside the classroom?

- If you wanted to add a border around the walls in your room, what would you need to know?

- At the store you can buy a 72-inch roll of border paper for $3.00. You can also buy the paper for $1.00 per yard. Which is the better deal?

Designing a Game

In this unit, you made measuring tools and estimated, measured, and compared lengths of different objects.

Use this new knowledge to design a game that uses measurements. You can use customary or metric units of measure.

1. First, decide on the goal of the game and write the game directions.

   - Think about what you want to measure, such as a jump, a roll, a toss, or something else.

   - How many players will play the game?

   - What will the players do? How do you win?

2. Next, decide on the materials needed to play the game.

   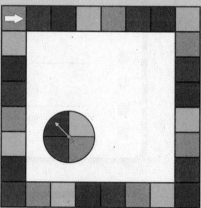

   - Will players need cards, spinners, or dot cubes?

   - Will players need something to toss, roll, or use as a placeholder?

   - Which measuring tools will players need?

3. Write a report about your project including some of the following:

   - What is the name of the game and what are the directions?

   - How big of an area do players need to play the game?

   - How will players use measurement in the game?

   - Include a drawing or sketch of your game.

UNIT J

Data, Graphs, and Probability

In this unit, I will:

- Find possible outcomes
- Tell whether something is more likely or less likely to happen
- Use different kinds of graphs to find information
- Collect and sort different kinds of graphs

Review Concepts
- scale
- survey

Projects
- Graph Scavenger Hunt
- Design a Survey and Graph

New Vocabulary

data   numbers or symbols sometimes collected from a *survey* or experiment to show information

equally likely   having the same chance of occurring

In a coin toss, you are equally likely to flip heads or tails.

graph   an organized drawing that shows sets of data and how they are related

impossible   an event that cannot happen; it has a probability of zero

It is impossible to choose white.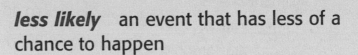

less likely   an event that has less of a chance to happen

more likely   an event that has more of a chance to happen

It is more likely you will choose a black tile.

outcome   a possible result of an experiment

pictograph   a graph that compares *data* by using picture symbols

Home Letter

English

During this math unit, your student will be exploring data, probability, and graphs. To help with learning, here are things to do at home.

- Look for graphs in newspapers, magazines, and on food cartons.
- Make graphs showing the number of phone calls your family receives each day or the number of hours your family watches television each day.
- Play games using number cubes or spinners and have your student tell you if rolling or spinning a certain number is more likely, less likely, or equally likely.

In class, your student will be:

- collecting samples of graphs;
- designing a survey and graph.

Español

Durante esta unidad de matemáticas, su estudiante va a explorar datos, probabilidades y gráficas. Para ayudar con el aprendizaje, sugerimos estas actividades para hacer en casa:

- Busque gráficas en periódicos, revistas y en las cajas de los alimentos empacados.
- Haga gráficas que indiquen el número de llamadas telefónicas que su familia recibe diariamente o el número de horas diarias que su familia ve televisión.
- Juegue con dados numéricos y flechas giratorias, y pídale a su estudiante que le diga si es más probable, menos probable o igualmente probable que el dado o la flecha giratoria caiga en un número determinado.

En clase, su estudiante va a:

- reunir muestras de gráficas;
- diseñar una encuesta y una gráfica.

Name: _____ Date: _____

Exploring Possible Outcomes

The coach for the Tigers softball team is assigning Katie, Mike, and Jamal to infield positions.

1. How many different ways can they play first-, second-, and third-base positions? Use the chart to record the different ways.

First Base	Second Base	Third Base

2. If Katie plays first base, what are the possible base assignments?

_____

_____

3. If Mike plays second base, what are the possible base assignments?

_____

_____

4. What multiplication sentence can you write that tells about all the possible combinations? _____

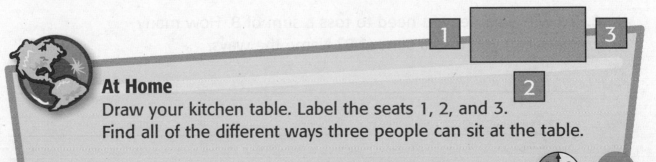

At Home
Draw your kitchen table. Label the seats 1, 2, and 3.
Find all of the different ways three people can sit at the table.

You are making sandwiches with turkey, lettuce, and tomatoes for your friends.

5. How many different ways can you layer the ingredients between the two slices of bread? Make a chart to record the possibilities and list them below.

_____

_____

_____

6. Martha wants lettuce on top of the turkey. How many ways can you make her sandwich? Name the ways.

_____

_____

7. Seth wants his tomatoes closest to the top slice of bread. How many ways can you make his sandwich? Name the ways.

_____

_____

We can also find combinations for number cubes. If you toss two number cubes, there are 5 ways to get a sum of 6.

| 1 and 5 | 2 and 4 | 3 and 3 |
| 5 and 1 | 4 and 2 | |

8. To win a game, you need to toss a sum of 8. How many ways can you toss a sum of 8? Name the ways.

_____

_____

Name: _____   Date: _____

Making Predictions

In the investigation, you pulled cubes from a bag. You predicted the color of the cube you would pull.

Copyright © Macmillan/McGraw-Hill, a division of The McGraw-Hill Companies, Inc.

It is *certain* that I will pull a white cube. It is *impossible* that I will pull a black cube.	It is *more likely* that I will pull a black cube. It is *less likely* that I will pull a white cube.	It is *equally likely* that I will pull a white cube or a black cube.

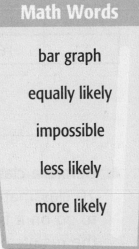

Math Words

bar graph

equally likely

impossible

less likely

more likely

Now, you will predict and record results of number cube tosses. Toss the cube four times to see what happens.

1. Use the terms *equally likely, less likely,* and *more likely* to predict what you think your tosses will be. Then record the results.

	Predict	**Toss 1**	**Toss 2**	**Toss 3**	**Toss 4**
Land on an even number					
Land on a number 2 through 6					
Land on number 3					

2. Compare your results to your predictions. What is the same? What is different?

_____

_____

3. Lucy pulled a shape from a bag and then replaced it 50 times. The table shows her results. Predict which bag she used. Explain why.

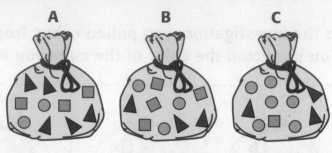

Circles	Triangles	Squares
31	16	3

---

4. Before a class vote, Martin asked 20 classmates where they wanted to go on a field trip. He showed the results of his survey on a pictograph.

Survey for Field Trip

Museum	🚌 🚌 🚌
Zoo	🚌 🚌 🚌 🚌 🚌
Park	🚌 🚌

Key: 🚌 = 2 students

Which place is most likely to win the class vote? Why?

---

5. Ask 10 students in your class where they would like to go on a class field trip. Use the same three choices. On a separate sheet of paper, make a pictograph representing their responses.

6. Use the data from your pictograph. Predict which place is most likely to win a class vote.

PROJECT

Graph Scavenger Hunt
Look on the pages of newspapers and magazines for different kinds of graphs. Can you find pictographs, bar graphs, and circle graphs? Make a class chart with all of the different kinds of graphs you can find. Organize the graphs by type.

ACTIVITY
J-3

Name: _____   Date: _____

Human Chart

In the investigation, you measured the width of your hand. Then you used that measurement to predict other measurements.

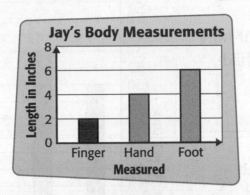

Compare Jay's measurements.

1. How much longer is his foot than his hand? _____ inches

2. How much longer is his foot than his finger? _____ inches

Now, make a bar graph showing your measurements.

3. Write your name in the graph title.

4. Color in the bars to show your measurements.

5. Compare your measurements. What do you find?

_____

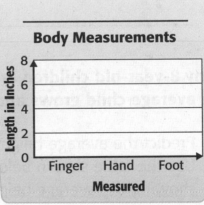

In Science
Drinking 8 glasses of water each day is a healthy habit. Record the number of glasses of water you drink for 3 days in a chart. Then make a graph showing the same information.

The bar graph to the right shows the average heights
of young children at different ages.

6. Look at the bar graph. How many
   inches are between each line?

   _____

7. According to this graph, about how
   many inches does a young child
   grow each year?

   _____

8. If the pattern continues, about
   how tall is a 4-year-old child?
   Color the bar.

   _____

9. About how much taller is a 4-year-
   old child than a 1-year-old child?

   _____

Heights of Young Children

Height in Inches

44
42
40
38
36
34
32
30
28
26
24
22
20
18
16
14
12
10
8
6
4
2
0

1 year 2 years 3 years 4 years

Age

Many 8-year-old children are about 50 inches tall.
The average child grows about 2 inches each year.

10. Predict the average heights of children from 8 years old to 12 years old.
    Use the table shown below to help you. Then, make a bar graph
    showing the average heights of children from 8 years old to 12 years old.

Age	8	9	10	11	12
Height in Inches	50	52			

Name: _____   Date: _____

Graphs: What Can You Interpret?

In the investigation, you interpreted a bar graph.
Now you will interpret a pictograph.

1. How many cans did each grade collect?

First grade: _____ cans

Second grade: _____ cans

Third grade: _____ cans

Fourth grade: _____ cans

Cans Collected in One Week

Fourth grade	🥫	🥫	🥫	🥫	🥫	
Third grade	🥫	🥫	🥫	🥫	🥫	🥫
Second grade	🥫	🥫	🥫			
First grade	🥫	🥫	🥫	🥫		

Key: 🥫 = 5 cans

2. Which grade collected the most cans? _____

3. How many more cans did the third grade collect than the second grade?

_____

4. How many cans were collected in all? _____ cans

5. Predict how many cans each grade will collect in two weeks.

First grade: _____ cans   Fourth grade: _____ cans

Second grade: _____ cans

Third grade: _____ cans

How Much Sugar and Salt?
Eating too much sugar and salt is unhealthy.
Compare the grams of sugar and salt (sodium)
on three containers of food. Make a chart and a graph to compare
the amounts. Talk about which foods are the most healthy and
which are the least healthy and why.

Maria asked students in her school what they liked to do most at recess. She created a bar graph with her survey results. What things do you know about the students in her school from the results?

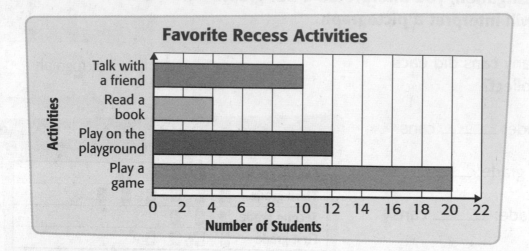

Favorite Recess Activities

6 Write the recess activities in order from the most favorite to the least favorite.

_____

_____

7. How many student responses are shown on the graph? _____

8. How many more students prefer to talk with a friend _____ than read a book?

9. Use the data from this chart. Make a pictograph that shows the same data.

Reflecting on What I Learned

New *Vocabulary* I learned:

1. _____

2. _____

3. _____

What did you learn about probability and prediction in this unit?

_____

_____

_____

List one relationship between a bar graph, data, and a scale that you learned.

_____

_____

Outside Your Classroom

Where will you see data, graphs, and probability outside the classroom?

- How likely is it that you will pick a green jelly bean from a bag of jelly beans?

- The teacher asks you and two friends to line up. In what different orders can you stand?

- You want to make a graph comparing the heights of the tallest animals. How will you make your graph?

Design a Survey and Graph

Use your knowledge of graphs and predictions to collect data from a survey and make your own graph.

1. First, create a survey. Ask classmates to take your survey and record their responses.

   - What question will you ask your classmates? What choices will they have?

   - How will you keep track of their responses? Will you use a chart? a list?

   - How many people will you ask? Who will you ask?

Favorite Season	
Season	**Number of People**
Winter	ЖHT III
Spring	IIII
Summer	ЖHT ЖHT
Fall	II

2. Next, create a graph that shows your data.

   - Will you make a bar graph or a pictograph?

   - What will be the scale of your graph?

3. Write a report about your project. Include some of the following:

   - What was your survey question? What were the response choices?

   - Whom did you survey?

   - Include your graph in the report. Describe one or two things you can interpret from your graph.

   - If you survey more classes, what do you think the results would be? Why?

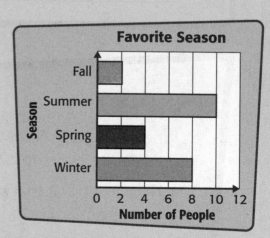

Acknowledgements

Teacher Edition Photo Credits

Cover Mazer Creative Services; United States coin images from the United States Mint; **A29** Ed-Imaging; **A33** Photolink/Getty Images; **A34** (t)image 100/CORBIS, (b)G.K. Vikki Hart/Getty Images; **A36** (t)C Squared Studios/Getty Images, (b)The McGraw-Hill Companies, Inc./Jacques Cornell photographer; **T45** Stockdisc/SuperStock.

Student Edition Photo Credits

i Thomas Northcut/Photodisc/Getty Images; **xiv** Rubberball/SuperStock; **xix** Getty Images; **xv** (l)C Squared Studios/Getty Images, (r)PhotoLink/Getty Images; **xvii** George Doyle/Stockbyte/Getty Images; **xviii** Mazer Creative Services; **xviii** Rubberball/Imagestate; **xx** Masterfile; **2** C Squared Studios/Getty Images; **3** (l)C Squared Studios/Getty Images, (c)Brand X Pictures/PunchStock, (r)Sean Justice/CORBIS; **7** Zave Smith/CORBIS; **8** Getty Images; **11** C Squared Studios/Getty Images; **12** Mazer Creative Services; **14** CORBIS; **15** Mazer Creative Services; **21** George Doyle/Stockbyte/Getty Images; **23, 25** Mazer Creative Services; **27** CORBIS; **28** Brand X Pictures/PunchStock; **31** Ed-Imaging; **33** Image Source/CORBIS; **34** Getty Images; **35** Mazer Creative Services; **36** Adrian Sherratt/Alamy; **38** (tl)Purestock/SuperStock, (tr)Brand X Pictures/PunchStock, (bl)Joseph Sohm/Visions of America, LLC/Alamy, (br)C Squared Studios/Photodisc/Getty Images; **43** Image Source Pink/Getty Images; **44** Masterfile; **45** (t)Stockdisc/SuperStock, (b)Digital Vision/Getty Images; **46** Mazer Creative Services; **47** (tl)Getty Images, (tc)C Squared Studios/Getty Images, (tr)The McGraw-Hill Companies, Inc./Jacques Cornell, (bl)Blend Images/Imagestate, (bc)Creatas/SuperStock, (br)Don Hammond/Design Pics/CORBIS; **49** Thomas Northcut/Photodisc/Getty Images; **50** (tl), (tc)Getty Images, (tr)Comstock/PunchStock, (bl)Photodisc, Inc./Getty Images, (br)Creatas/PunchStock; **53** Rubberball/SuperStock; **55** Ryan McVay/Photodisc/Getty Images; **57** Mazer Creative Services; **58** (t)Comstock/PunchStock, (b)The McGraw-Hill Companies, Inc./Jacques Cornell; **66** Junophoto/fStop/Getty Images; **68** (t)The McGraw-Hill Companies Inc./Ken Cavanagh, (b)Lawrence Manning/CORBIS; **72** (tl)Lawrence Manning/CORBIS, (tr)C Squared Studios/Getty Images, (others) Mazer Creative Services; **73** (l)Ross Whitaker/Getty Images, (r)WireImageStock/Masterfile; **75, 77** Mazer Creative Services; **81** Ed-Imaging; **88** Mazer Creative Services; **89** (l)PhotoLink/Getty Images, (c)The McGraw-Hill Companies, Inc./Jacques Cornell, (r)The McGraw-Hill Companies; **90** (t)C Squared Studios/Getty Images, (b)The McGraw-Hill Companies; **91** (tl), (tr)Mazer Creative Services, (cl), (cr)Masterfile, (bl)The McGraw-Hill Companies, Inc/Ken Karp, (br)Maria Taglienti-Molinari/Brand X/CORBIS; **93** (t)Maria Taglienti-Molinari/Brand X/CORBIS, (b)Rubberball/Imagestate; **94** (t to b)Brand X Pictures/PunchStock, (2)Thomas Northcut/Digital Vision/Getty Images, (3)curved-light/Alamy, (4)Comstock Select/CORBIS; **105** Ryan McVay/Photodisc/Getty Images; **107** Mazer Creative Services.

Glossary/Glosario

Math Online ▶ A mathematics multilingual glossary is available at www.macmillanmh.com. The glossary includes the following languages.

Arabic	Cantonese	Korean	Tagalog
Bengali	English	Russian	Urdu
Brazilian	Haiti Creole	Spanish	Vietnamese
Portuguese	Hmong		

Cómo usar el glosario en español:

1. Busca el término en inglés que desces encontrar.
2. El término en español, junto con la definición, se encuentran en la columna de la derecha.

A

addend   Any numbers being added to together.

add (adding, addition)   An operation on two or more *addends* that results in a *sum*.

$$9 + 3 = 12$$

angle   A figure that is formed by two *rays* with the same *endpoint*.

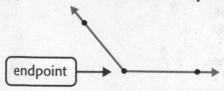

area   The number of *square units* needed to cover the inside of a region or plane figure.

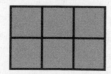

area = 6 square units

---

sumando   Cualquier número que se le suma a otro.

suma (sumar, adición)   Operación que se realiza en dos o más *sumandos* y que resulta en una *suma*.

$$9 + 3 = 12$$

ángulo   Figura formada por dos *rayos* con el mismo *extremo*.

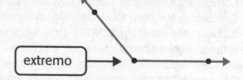

área   Número de *unidades cuadradas* necesarias para cubrir el interior de una región o figura plana.

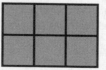

área = 6 unidades cuadradas

Glossary/Glosario

array Objects or symbols displayed in rows of the same length and columns of the same length.

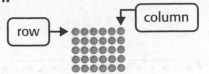

arreglo Objetos o símbolos representados en filas de la misma longitud y columnas de la misma longitud.

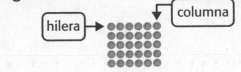

Associative Property of Addition The property which states that the grouping of the *addends* does not change the *sum*.

$$(4 + 5) + 2 = 4 + (5 + 2)$$

propiedad asociativa de la adición Propiedad que establece que la agrupación de los *sumandos* no altera la *suma*.

$$(4 + 5) + 2 = 4 + (5 + 2)$$

Associative Property of Multiplication The property which states that the grouping of the factors does not change the *product*.

$$3 \times (6 \times 2) = (3 \times 6) \times 2$$

propiedad asociativa de la multiplicación Propiedad que establece que la agrupación de los factores no altera el producto.

$$3 \times (6 \times 2) = (3 \times 6) \times 2$$

B

bar graph A graph that compares *data* by using bars of different lengths or heights to show the values.

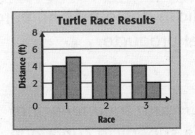

gráfica de barras Gráfica que compara los datos usando barras de distintas longitudes o alturas para mostrar los valores.

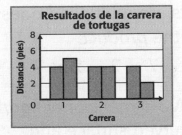

base One of two parallel congruent faces in a prism.

base Una de dos caras congruentes paralelas en un prisma.

benchmark A number used as a guide for making an estimate.

número de referencia Número que se usa como guía para hacer una estimación.

capacity The amount a container can hold, measured in units of dry or liquid measure.

capacidad Cantidad de material líquido o seco que puede contener un envase.

centimeter (cm) A *metric unit* for measuring *length and height*.

100 centimeters = 1 meter

centímetro (cm) Unidad métrica de longitud y altura.

100 centímetros = 1 metro

Commutative Property of Addition The property that states that the order in which two numbers are added does not change the *sum*.

12 + 15 = 15 + 12

propiedad conmutativa de la adición Propiedad que establece que el orden en el cual se suman dos o más números no altera la *suma*.

12 + 15 = 15 + 12

Commutative Property of Multiplication The property that states that the order in which two numbers are multiplied does not change the *product*.

7 × 2 = 2 × 7

propiedad conmutativa de la multiplicación Propiedad que establece que el orden en el cual se multiplican dos o más números no altera el producto.

7 × 2 = 2 × 7

cone A *3-dimensional figure* with a curved surface and a circular base which comes to a point called the *vertex.*

cono *Figura tridimensional* con una superficie curva que conecta la base circular con un punto llamado vértice.

congruent figures Two figures having the same size and the same shape.

cube A *3-dimensional* figure with six faces that are congruent.

cubic unit A unit for measuring *volume,* such as a cubic inch or a cubic centimeter.

cup (c) A customary unit for measuring *capacity*.

   1 cup = 8 ounces
16 cups = 1 gallon

customary system The measurement system that includes units such as foot, pound, quart, and degrees Fahrenheit. Also called *standard measurement.*

cylinder A *3-dimensional figure* having two circular *bases* and a curved surface connecting the two *bases.*

---

congruentes figuras Dos figuras con la misma forma y el mismo tamaño.

cubo Figura *tridimensional* con seis caras cuadradas *congruentes.*

unidad cúbica Unidad de *volumen,* como la pulgada cúbica o el centímetro cúbico.

taza (c) Unidad inglesa de *capacidad*.

   1 taza = 8 onzas
16 tazas = 1 galón

sistema inglés Sistema de medición que incluye unidades como el pie, la libra, el cuarto de galón y los grados Fahrenheit. También llamado medición estándar.

cilindro *Figura tridimensional* que tiene dos bases circulares y una superficie curva que une las dos bases.

D

---

data Numbers or symbols sometimes collected from a *survey* or experiment to show information. Datum is singular; data is plural.

datos Números o símbolos, algunas veces recolectados de una *encuesta* o un experimento, para mostrar información.

decimal A number with one or more digits to the right of the decimal point, such as 8.37 or 0.05.

número decimal Número con uno o más dígitos a la derecha del punto decimal, como 8.37 o 0.05.

decimal point A period separating the ones and the *tenths* in a decimal number.

0.8 or $3.77

punto decimal Punto que separa las unidades de las *décimas* en un número decimal.

0.8 o $3.77

decimeter (dm) A metric unit for measuring length and height.

1 decimeter = 10 centimeters

decímetro (dm) Unidad métrica para medir longitud y altura.

1 decímeter = 10 centímetros

denominator The bottom number in a *fraction*.

In $\frac{5}{6}$, 6 is the denominator.

denominador El número inferior en una *fracción*.

En $\frac{5}{6}$, 6 es el denominador.

difference The answer to a *subtraction* problem.

diferencia Respuesta a un problema de *sustracción*.

digit A symbol used to write numbers. The ten digits are 0, 1, 2, 3, 4, 5, 6, 7, 8, and 9.

dígito Símbolo que se usa para escribir números. Los diez dígitos son 0, 1, 2, 3, 4, 5, 6, 7, 8, 9.

divide (division) To separate into equal groups.

dividir (división) Separar en grupos iguales.

dividend A number that is being divided.

$3\overline{)9}$ 9 is the dividend

dividendo El número que se divide.

$3\overline{)9}$ 9 es el dividendo

divisor The number by which the dividend is being divided.

$3\overline{)19}$ 3 is the divisor

divisor Número entre el cual se divide el dividendo.

$3\overline{)19}$ 3 es el divisor

dollar ($) One dollar = 100¢ or 100 cents. Also written as $1.00.

dólar ($) Un dólar = 100¢ o 100 centavos. También se escribe como $1.00.

front

back

frente

revés

edge The line segment where two faces of a solid figure meet.

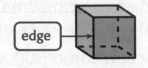

equally likely Having the same chance of occurring.

In a coin toss, you are equally likely to flip heads or tails.

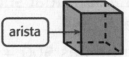

equals sign (=) A symbol of equality.

equation A sentence that contains an equals sign (=), showing that two expressions are equal.

$$5 + 7 = 12$$

equilateral triangle A *triangle* with three *sides* of the same *length*.

equivalent fractions *Fractions* that have the same value.

$$\frac{2}{4} = \frac{1}{2}$$

estimate A number close to an exact value. An estimate indicates *about* how much.

$$47 + 22 \text{ is about } 70.$$

arista Segmento de recta donde concurren dos caras de una figura sólida.

equiprobable Que tienen la misma posibilidad de ocurrir.

Al lanzar una moneda, tienes la misma posibilidad de que caiga cara o cruz.

signo de igualdad (=) Que tiene el mismo valor que o que es igual a.

ecuación Expresión que contiene un signo de igualdad y que muestra dos espresiones son iguales.

$$5 + 7 = 12$$

triángulo equilátero *Triángulo* con tres *lados* de la misma *longitud*.

fracciones equivalentes *Fracciones* que tienen el mismo valor.

$$\frac{2}{4} \text{ y } \frac{1}{2}$$

estimación Número cercano a un valor exacto. Una estimación indica aproximadamente cuánto.

$$47 + 22 \text{ es aproximadamente } 70.$$

event   A set of *outcomes* in a *probability* experiment.

expanded form/expanded notation   The representation of a number as a sum that shows the value of each digit.

536 is written as 500 + 30 + 6.

expression   A combination of numbers and operations.

5 + 7

evento   Conjunto de *resultados* de un experimento *probabilístico*.

forma desarrollada/notación desarrollada   Representación de un número como suma que muestra el valor de cada dígito.

536 se escribe como 500 + 30 + 6.

expresión   Combinación de números y símbolos.

5 + 7

face   The flat part of a 3-dimensional figure.

A square is a face of a cube.

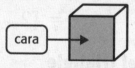

fact family   A group of *related facts* using the same numbers.

5 + 3 = 8	15 × 3 = 15
3 + 5 = 8	13 × 5 = 15
8 − 3 = 5	15 ÷ 5 = 13
8 − 5 = 3	15 ÷ 3 = 15

factor   A number that divides a whole number evenly. Also a number that is multiplied by another number.

cara   La parte llana de una figura tridimensional.

Un cuadrado es una cara de un cubo.

familia de operaciones   Grupo de *operaciones relacionadas* que usan los mismos números.

5 + 3 = 8	15 × 3 = 15
3 + 5 = 8	13 × 5 = 15
8 − 3 = 5	15 ÷ 5 = 13
8 − 5 = 3	15 ÷ 3 = 15

factor   Número que divide exactamente a otro número entero. También es un número multiplicado por otro número.

flip (reflection) An figure that is flipped over a line to create a mirror image of the figure.

foot (ft) A *customary unit* for measuring *length*. Plural is feet.

$$1 \text{ foot} = 12 \text{ inches}$$

fraction A number that represents part of a whole or part of a set.

$$\frac{1}{2}, \frac{1}{3}, \frac{1}{4}, \frac{3}{4}$$

frequency The number of times a result occurs or something happens in a set amount of time or collection of data.

function A relationship in which one quantity depends upon another quantity.

function table A table of ordered pairs that is based on a rule.

flip (reflexión) Figura que se vuelca sobre una línea para crear una imagen especular de la figura.

pie (pie) Unidad inglesa de *longitud*.

$$1 \text{ pie} = 12 \text{ pulgadas}$$

fracción Número que representa parte de un todo o parte de un conjunto.

$$\frac{1}{2}, \frac{1}{3}, \frac{1}{4}, \frac{3}{4}$$

frecuencia El número de veces que ocurre un resultado o sucede algo en un período de tiempo dado o en una colección de datos.

función Relación en que una cantidad depende de otra cantidad.

tabla de funciones Tabla de pares ordenados que se basa en una regla.

gallon (gal) A *customary unit* for measuring *capacity* for liquids.

$$1 \text{ gallon} = 4 \text{ quarts}$$

gram (g) A *metric unit* for measuring *mass*.

galón (gal) Unidad de medida inglesa de *capacidad* líquida.

$$1 \text{ galón} = 4 \text{ cuartos}$$

gramo (g) Unidad métrica de *masa*.

graph An organized drawing that shows sets of data and how they are related to each other. Also a type of chart.

a bar graph

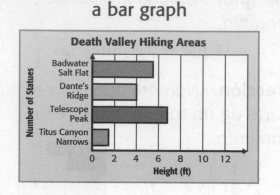

gráfica Dibujo organizado que muestra conjuntos de datos y cómo se relacionan. También, un tipo de diagrama.

una gráfica de barras

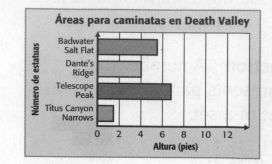

H

height The distance from bottom to top.

altura Distancia de la parte inferior a la superior.

hexagon A *polygon* with six *sides* and six *angles*.

hexágono *Polígono* con seis *lados* y seis *ángulos*.

hour (h) A unit of time equal to 60 *minutes*.

1 hour = 60 minutes

hora (h) Unidad de tiempo igual a 60 minutos.

1 hora = 60 minutos

hundredth A place value position. One of one hundred equal parts.

In the number 0.05, the number 5 is in the hundredths place.

centésima Valor de posición. Una de cien partes iguales.

En el número 0.05, 5 está en el lugar de las centésimas.

Identity Property of Addition
If you add zero to a number, the sum is the same as the given number.

$$3 + 0 = 3 \text{ or } 0 + 3 = 3$$

Identity Property of Multiplication
If you multiply a number by 1, the product is the same as the given number.

$$8 \times 1 = 8 = 8 \times 1$$

impossible   An event that cannot happen. It has a probability of zero.

It is impossible to choose red.

inch (in.)   A *customary unit* for measuring *length*. Plural is inches.

inequality   A number sentence that uses < (less than) or > (greater than).

inverse operation   Operations that undo each other.
Addition and subtraction are inverse or opposite operations. Multiplication and division are also inverse operations.

propiedad de identidad de la adición   Si sumas cero a un número, la suma es igual al número dado.

$$3 + 0 = 3 \text{ o } 0 + 3 = 3$$

propiedad de identidad de la multiplicación   Si multiplicas un número por 1, el producto es igual al número dado.

$$8 \times 1 = 8 = 8 \times 1$$

imposible   Evento que no puede suceder, el cual tiene probabilidad cero.

Es imposible elegir rojo.

pulgada (pulg)   *Unidad inglesa* de *longitud*. El plural es pulgadas.

desigualdad   Expresión numérica que usa < (menor que), > (mayor que), ≤ (menor que o igual a), o ≥ (mayor que o igual a).

operación inversa   Operaciones que se anulan entre sí.
La adición y la sustracción son operaciones inversas u opuestas. La multiplicación y la división también son operaciones inversas.

is greater than > An inequality relationship showing that the value on the left of the symbol is greater than the value on the right.

$5 > 3$ 5 is greater than 3

is less than < The value on the left side of the symbol is smaller than the value on the right side.

$4 < 7$ 4 is less than 7

isosceles triangle
A *triangle* with 2 *sides* of the same *length*.

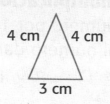
4 cm   4 cm
3 cm

es mayor que > Relación de desigualdad que muestra que el número a la izquierda del símbolo es mayor que el número a la derecha.

$5 > 3$ 5 es mayor que 3

es menor que < El número a la izquierda del símbolo es más pequeño que el número a la derecha.

$4 < 7$ 4 es menor que 7

triángulo isósceles
Triángulo que tiene por lo menos 2 *lados* del mismo *largo*.

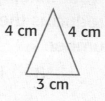
4 cm   4 cm
3 cm

K

key   Tells what or how many each symbol stands for.

kilogram (kg)   A *metric unit* for measuring mass.

kilometer (km)   A *metric unit* for measuring length.

clave   Indica qué significa o cuánto vale cada símbolo.

kilogramo (kg)   *Unidad métrica de masa.*

kilómetro (km)   *Unidad métrica de longitud.*

L

length   Measurement of the distance between two points.

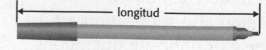
length

less likely   An event that has less of a chance to happen.

longitud   Medida de la distancia entre dos puntos.

longitud

menos probable   Evento que tiene una posibilidad menor de ocurrir.

likely An event that will probably happen.

It is likely you will choose a red tile.

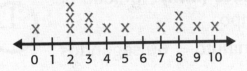

line plot A graph that uses columns of Xs above a *number line* to show frequency of data.

liter (L) A *metric unit* for measuring *volume* or *capacity*.

1 liter = 1,000 milliliters

posible Evento que probablemente sucederá.

Es posible que elijas un cubo rojo.

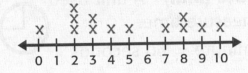

esquema lineal Gráfica que usa columnas de X sobre una *recta numérica* para representar frecuencias de datos.

litro (L) Unidad *métrica* de *volumen* o *capacidad*.

1 litro = 1,000 mililitros

mass The amount of matter in an object. Two examples of units of measure would be gram and kilogram.

meter (m) A *metric unit* for measuring *length*.

1 meter = 100 centimeters

metric system (SI) The measurement system based on powers of 10 that includes units such as meter, gram, and liter.

mile (mi) A *customary unit* of measure for distance.

1 mile = 5,280 feet

masa Cantidad de materia de un cuerpo. Dos ejemplos de unidades de medida son la libra y el kilogramo.

metro (m) *Unidad métrica* de *longitud*.

1 metro = 100 centímetros

sistema métrico (sm) Sistema de medición que se basa en potencias de 10 y que incluye unidades como el metro, gramo, y litro.

milla (mi) *Unidad inglesa* de distancia.

1 milla = 5,280 pies

milliliter (mL) A *metric unit* used for measuring *capacity*.

1,000 milliliters = 1 liter

mililitro (ml) *Unidad métrica de capacidad.*

1,000 mililitros = 1 litro

millimeter (mm) A *metric unit* used for measuring *length*.

1,000 millimeters = 1 meter

milímetro (mm) *Unidad métrica de longitud.*

1,000 milímetros = 1 metro

minute (min) A unit used to measure time.

1 minute = 60 seconds

minuto (min) Unidad de tiempo.

1 minuto = 60 segundos

more likely An event that has more of a chance to happen.

It is more likely you will choose a black tile.

más probable Evento que tiene una posibilidad mayor de ocurrir.

Es probable que escojas una ficha negra.

multiples A multiple of a number is the *product* of that number and any whole number.

15 is a multiple of 5 because $3 \times 5 = 15$.

múltiplos Un múltiplo de un número es el *producto* de ese número por cualquier número entero.

15 es un múltiplo de 5 porque $3 \times 5 = 15$.

multiplication An operation on two numbers to find their product. It can be thought of as repeated *addition*.

$3 \times 4 = 12$
$4 + 4 + 4 = 12$

multiplicación Operación de adición repetida del mismo número.

$3 \times 4 = 12$
$4 + 4 + 4 = 12$

multiply To find the product of 2 or more numbers.

multiplicar (multiplicación) Calcular el producto.

number line   A line with number labels.

number sentence   An expression using numbers and the = sign, or the < or > sign.

$$5 + 4 = 9; 8 > 5$$

numerator   The number above the bar in a *fraction*; the part of the fraction that tells how many of the equal parts are being used.

recta numéricarecta numérica
Recta con rótulos de números.

enunciado numérico   Expresión que usa números y el signo = o los signos < y >.

$$5 + 4 = 9; 8 > 5$$

numerador   Número que está encima de la barra de *fracción*; la parte de la fracción que indica cuántas partes iguales se están usando.

octagon   A *polygon* with eight *sides*.

operation   A mathematical process such as addition (+), subtraction (−), multiplication (×), and division (÷).

ounce (oz) ounces   A *customary unit* for measuring *weight* or *capacity*.

outcome   A possible result of an experiment.

octágono   *Polígono* de 8 *lados*.

operación   Proceso matemático como la adición (+), la sustracción (−), la multiplicación (×), la división (÷).

onza (oz)   *Unidad inglesa* de peso o *capacidad*.

resultado   Resultado posible de un experimento.

Glossary/Glosario

parallel Lines that are the same distance apart. Parallel lines do not meet.

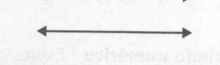

parallelogram A quadrilateral with four sides in which each pair of opposite sides are parallel and equal in length.

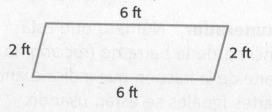

pattern A sequence of numbers, figures, or symbols that follows a rule or design.

2, 4, 6, 8, 10

pentagon A *polygon* with five *sides*.

perimeter The *distance* around a shape or region.

pictograph A graph that compares *data* by using picture symbols.

Books Read During Read-A-Thon

Anita	
David	
Emma	
Jonah	
Mary	
Sam	

rectas paralelas Rectas separadas por la misma distancia. Las rectas paralelas no se intersecan.

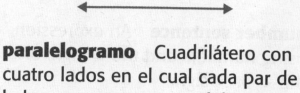

paralelogramo Cuadrilátero con cuatro lados en el cual cada par de lados opuestos son paralelos y de la misma longitud.

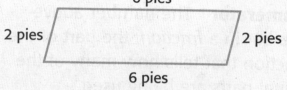

patrón Sucesión de números, figuras, o símbolos que sigue una regla o un diseño.

2, 4, 6, 8, 10

pentágono *Polígono* de cinco *lados*.

perímetro *Distancia* alrededor de una figura o región.

pictograma Gráfica que compara *datos* usando figuras.

Libros leídos durante el maratón de lectura

Anita	
David	
Emma	
Jonah	
Mary	
Sam	

Glossary/Glosario

pint (pt) A *customary unit* for measuring *capacity*.

    1 pint = 2 cups

place value The value given to a *digit* by its place in a number.

point An exact location in space. Also refers to a decimal place.

polygon A closed plane figure formed using line segments that meet only at their endpoints.

pound (lb) A *customary unit* for measuring *weight*.

    1 pound = 16 ounces.

prism A 3-*dimensional figure* with two parallel, congruent polygons as bases and parallelograms for faces.

probability The chance that an event will happen.

product The answer to a multiplication problem.

---

pinta (pt) *Unidad inglesa* de capacidad.

    1 pinta = 2 tazas

valor de posición El valor de un *dígito* según su lugar en el número.

punto Ubicación exacta en el espacio. También se refiere a un lugar decimal.

polígono Figura plana cerrada formada por segmentos de recta que sólo concurren en sus extremos.

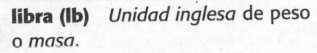

libra (lb) *Unidad inglesa* de peso o *masa*.

    1 libra = 16 onzas

prisma *Figura tridimensional* con dos polígonos paralelos y congruentes como bases y paralelogramos como caras.

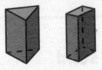

probabilidad La posibilidad de que ocurra un evento.

producto Respuesta a un problema de multiplicación.

quadrilateral   A shape that has 4 sides and 4 angles.

square, rectangle, and parallelogram

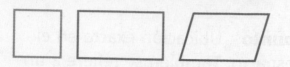

cuadrilátero   Figura con 4 lados y 4 ángulos.

cuadrado, rectángulo y paralelogramo

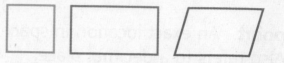

quart (qt)   A *customary unit* for measuring *capacity*.

1 quart = 4 cups

cuarto (ct)   *Unidad inglesa* de *capacidad*.

1 cuarto = 4 tazas

quotient   The answer to a *division problem*.

15 ÷ 3 = 5   ← 5 is the quotient

cociente   Respuesta a un *problema de división*.

15 ÷ 3 = 5   ← 5 es el cociente

R

rectangle   A *quadrilateral* with four *right angles*; opposite *sides* are equal length and *parallel*.

rectángulo   *Cuadrilátero* con cuatro *ángulos rectos*; los *lados* opuestos son iguales y *paralelos*.

rectangular solid
A 3-*dimensional figure* with six faces that are rectangles.

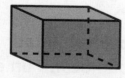

prisma rectangular
Figura tridimensional con seis caras rectangulares.

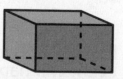

regroup   To use place value to exchange equal amounts when renaming a number.

reagrupar   Usar el valor de posición para intercambiar cantidades iguales cuando se convierte un número.

Glossary/Glosario

related fact(s)   Basic facts using the same numbers. Sometimes called a fact family.

$$4 + 1 = 5 \quad | \quad 5 \times 6 = 30$$
$$1 + 4 = 5 \quad | \quad 6 \times 5 = 30$$
$$5 - 4 = 1 \quad | \quad 30 \div 5 = 6$$
$$5 - 1 = 4 \quad | \quad 30 \div 6 = 5$$

rhombus   A *parallelogram* with four *sides* of the same *length*.

round   To change the *value* of a number to one that is easier to work with. To find the nearest value of a number based on a given place value.

27 rounded to the nearest 10 is 30.

operación (u operaciones relacionada(s)   Operaciones básicas que usan los mismos números. A veces llamadas familia de operaciones.

$$4 + 1 = 5 \quad | \quad 5 \times 6 = 30$$
$$1 + 4 = 5 \quad | \quad 6 \times 5 = 30$$
$$5 - 4 = 1 \quad | \quad 30 \div 5 = 6$$
$$5 - 1 = 4 \quad | \quad 30 \div 6 = 5$$

rombo   *Paralelogramo* con cuatro *lados* del mismo *largo*.

redondear   Cambiar el *valor* de un número por uno con el que es más fácil trabajar. Calcular el valor más cercano de un número en base a un valor de posición dado.

27 redondeado a la décima más cercana es 30.

(S)

scale   Equally spaced marks along an axis of a graph.

similar   Two figures that have the same shape but are not the same size.

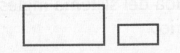

simplest form   A fraction in which the numerator and the denominator have no common factor greater than 1.

$\frac{3}{5}$ is the simplest form of $\frac{6}{10}$.

escala   Conjunto de números igualmente separados en un lado de una gráfica.

similar   Dos figuras que tienen la misma forma pero que no tienen el mismo tamaño.

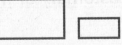

forma reducida   *Fracción en que el numerador y el denominador no tienen un factor común* mayor que 1.

$\frac{3}{5}$ es la forma reducida de $\frac{6}{10}$.

skip count To count forward or backward by a given number or in intervals of a number.

Example: 3, 6, 9, 12 …

slide (translation) Sliding a figure in a straight line horizontally, vertically, or diagonally.

solid figure A solid figure having the three dimensions: length, width, and height.

sphere A 3-*dimensional figure* that has the shape of a round ball.

square A rectangle with four *congruent sides*.

square number The product of a number multiplied by itself.

Example: $5^2 = 5 \times 5 = 25$
25 is a square number.

standard form/standard notation The usual way of writing a number that shows only its *digits*, no words.

537   89   1,642

standard units Measuring units from the customary or metric system.

subtraction (subtract) An operation that tells the difference, when some or all are taken away.

$9 - 4 = 5$

---

conteo salteado Contar hacia adelante o hacia atrás por un número dado o en intervalos de un número.

Ejemplo: 3, 6, 9, 12, …

slide (traslación) Deslizar una figura horizontal, vertical o diagonalmente en línea recta.

figura sólida Figura sólida tridimensional: largo, ancho y alto.

esfera *Figura tridimensional* con forma de pelota redonda.

cuadrado Rectángulo con cuatro *lados congruentes*.

número al cuadrado Producto de un número multiplicado por sí mismo.

Ejemplo: $5^2 = 5 \times 5 = 25$
25 es un número cuadrado.

forma estándar/notación estándar La manera habitual de escribir un número que sólo muestra sus dígitos, sin palabras.

537   89   1,642

unidades estándar Unidades de medida del sistema inglés o del métrico.

resta (sustracción) Operación que indica la diferencia cuando se elimina algo o todo.

$9 - 4 = 5$

sum   The answer to an addition problem.

$$8 + 5 = 13$$

survey   A method of collecting data.

symmetry   An object has line symmetry if one side is the mirror image of the other side.

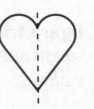

suma   Respuesta a un problema de adición.

$$8 + 5 = 13$$

encuesta   Un método para reunir datos.

simetría   Un objeto tiene un eje de simetría si uno de sus lados es la imagen de espejo del otro lado.

T

table   A way to organize and display data with rows and columns.

tally chart   A way to keep track of data using tally marks to record the results.

What is Your Favorite Color?	
Color	Tally
Blue	ℍℍ |||
Green	||||

tally mark(s)   A mark made to keep track and display data recorded from a survey.

tenth   One of ten equal parts or $\frac{1}{10}$.

tabla   Manera de organizar y representar datos con filas y columnas.

tabla de conteo   Una manera de llevar la cuenta de los datos usando marcas de conteo para anotar los resultados.

¿Cuál es tu color favorito?	
Color	Conteo
Azul	ℍℍ |||
Verde	||||

marcas(s) de conteo   Marca hecha para llevar la cuenta y presentar datos reunidos con una encuesta.

décima   Una de diez partes iguales o $\frac{1}{10}$.

thousand(s)   A place value of a number.

In 1,253, the **1** is in the thousands place.

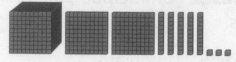

millares   Valor de posición de un número.

1,233, el **1** está en el lugar de las unidades de millar.

three-dimensional figure   A solid figure that has *length*, *width*, and *height*.

figura tridimensional   Figura sólida que tiene *largo*, *ancho* y *alto*.

trapezoid   A four-sided plane shape with only two opposite sides that are the same length.

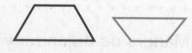

trapecio   Figura de cuatro lados con sólo dos lados opuestos que tienen la misma longitud.

triangle   A *polygon* with three sides and three angles.

triángulo   *Polígono* con tres lados y tres ángulos.

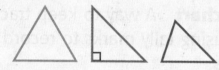

turn (rotation)   Rotating a figure about a point.

turn (rotación)   Rotar una figura alrededor de un punto.

two-dimensional figure   The outline of a shape, such as a triangle, square, or rectangle, which has only *length*, *width*, and *area*. Also called a plane figure.

figura bidimensional   El contorno de una figura, como un triángulo, un cuadrado o un rectángulo, que sólo tiene *largo*, *ancho* y *área*. También se llama figura plana.

unit cost   The price of a single piece or item.

costo unitario   El precio de una sola pieza o artículo.

unlikely An event that will probably *not* happen.

It is unlikely you will choose a yellow tile.

improbable Evento que probablemente *no* sucederá.

Es imporbable que elijas una baldosa amarilla.

volume The number of cubic units needed to fill a 3-*dimensional figure* or solid figure.

volumen Número de unidades cúbicas necesarias para llenar una *figura tridimensional* o sólida.

weight A measurement that tells how heavy an object is.

peso Medida que indica la pesadez de un cuerpo.

whole number The numbers 0, 1, 2, 3, 4 ...

número entero Los números 0, 1, 2, 3, 4 ...

yard (yd) A *customary unit* for measuring *length*.

  1 yard = 3 feet or 36 inches

yarda (yd) *Medida inglesa* de *longitud*.

  1 yarda = 3 pies o 36 pulgadas

Zero Property of Multiplication The property that states any number multiplied by zero is zero.

  $0 \times 5 = 0$ $5 \times 0 = 0$

propiedad del producto nulo de la multiplicación Propiedad que establece que cualquier número multiplicado por cero es igual a cero.

  $0 \times 5 = 0$ $5 \times 0 = 0$